Sarah Bartlett is a professional astrologer with over twenty years' experience. She has written many mind, body and spirit books including the international best-sellers *The Little Book of Practical Magic, The Tarot Bible, The Witch's Spellbook, The Secrets of the Universe in 100 Symbols* and *National Geographic Guide to the World's Supernatural Places*. Sarah lives in the magical countryside of the Isle of Wight.

Sarah Bartlett

The Little Book of Moon Magic

Working with the power of the lunar cycles

PIATKUS

PIATKUS

First published in Great Britain in 2020 by Piatkus

1 3 5 7 9 10 8 6 4 2

A CIP catalogue record for this book
is available from the British Library.

ISBN 978-0-349-42564-1

Typeset in Perpetua by M Rules
Printed and bound in Great Britain by
Clays Ltd, Elcograf S.p.A.

Papers used by Piatkus are from well-managed forests
and other responsible sources.

MIX
Paper from
responsible sources
FSC® C104740

Piatkus
An imprint of
Little, Brown Book Group
Carmelite House
50 Victoria Embankment
London EC4Y 0DZ

An Hachette UK Company
www.hachette.co.uk

www.littlebrown.co.uk

To Jess, and all who wish on the Moon.

Contents

Contents

PART THREE

Moon Signs

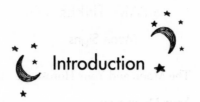

Introduction

The Moon is our closest 'heavenly sphere' of wonder, mystery and magic. She has been held in awe, worshipped, venerated and glorified in every civilisation since the dawn of mankind. Along with the Sun, planets and stars observed by ancient peoples in their religious mythologies, the Moon has not only been treasured as a source of divine power and mysterious influence, but has also shaped our sense of time and our awareness of the striking difference between day and night.

The movements of the Moon and Sun have also determined our perception of the seasons and how the Moon's cycle can be put to positive use: for example, when to sow and when to harvest. More importantly, we cannot forget the Moon's influence on the Earth's tides, and her apparent effect on our moods and feelings, and on astrological charts.

In fact, the mystical nature of the Moon has permeated our beliefs and been embraced by most cultures in our quest for further understanding. What can we learn from the Moon, and what can she teach us about ourselves?

*

This little book is filled with secret ways to connect you to the magic of the Moon's power. By using enchantments, rituals, astrology, spells, crystals and affirmations, you will discover how to draw down and maximise this potent lunar energy at the most auspicious times, to make your life what you truly want it to be. From wishing on the Moon and manifesting success to knowing when to attract new romance, this guide reveals how to go with the flow of the Moon in order to bring you the happiness you seek.

We will also explore how to track and utilise astrological lunar cycles for self-improvement, as well as how to work with lunar energy for positive transformation. You will also discover how your Moon sign determines your moods, comfort zones and emotional needs, and so come to understand the kind of partner you feel most at home with. You will learn how to work with your Moon sign in tandem with the Moon's phases for well-being and harmony in the home.

Finally, we're going to look at how to utilise the power of the dark side of the Moon, symbolised by what is known as the 'Black Moon Lilith'. Here you will discover the hidden aspects of yourself and your true sexual needs according to the sign in which the Black Moon is placed in your chart, along with an empowerment ritual to be performed in the correct lunar cycle.

With this kind of lunar awareness, you can honour your own authentic self for positive transformation and reconnect to the power of nature. After all, the Moon, Earth, tides and everything on this planet are all part of a greater web, of which you too are part. As the Moon engages with the energy of the Earth, so Mother Nature responds to her influence. Thus, by giving out the best of yourself to the universe, you help to heal and promote goodness throughout the natural world too.

So, whether you seek emotional healing, spiritual growth or a sense of being at one with nature, this book will give you all the tools you need to channel the Moon's power, whenever you need it, and to be the best you.

PART ONE

Lunar Power

'The earth together with its
surrounding waters must in fact have
such a shape as its shadow reveals, for
it eclipses the moon with the arc of a
perfect circle.'

COPERNICUS

Whether in magic work, astrology, folklore or traditional time tracking (using the position of the Moon to determine the day, month or year), lunar phases have been used throughout history by astrologers, ancient priestesses, magicians and chroniclers to mirror not only our own human cycle of life and death, but our spiritual or personal quest for a sense of self, too. The Moon weaves a spell upon us with her changing face in the sky, and it is this forever changing but constant cycle that we can use to weave and cast our own magic and spells.

The Moon waxes, or grows larger, until she becomes a glowing silver-white orb. Then, night by night, she wanes, or shrinks, to a curved crescent on the opposite side, until she disappears altogether. A few days later, a fine, slender crescent Moon appears again on the waxing side. This endless cycle mirrors our own growing desires and waning disappointments. By understanding these phases and their impact on our psyche and our innate connection to nature, we can work to improve and empower ourselves in every aspect of our lives.

Before we learn how to do this, let's look briefly at the so-called facts that support various theories and certainties about the familiar lunar landscape. Although this book is dedicated to using the magical energy of the Moon, there is some key information we need to consider so we can see the Moon's mystique in her true light.

Chapter 1

Who's Shot

Science and Fact

Chapter 1

Who is She?
Science and Fact

In the medieval to Renaissance period, when the Catholic Church believed that the Earth was flat, and anyone who said it was otherwise was thought to be a heretic, it's hardly surprising that the astronomer and philosopher Copernicus was mocked and scorned. His apt observations about lunar and solar eclipses not only confirmed his heliocentric theory, and his studies of the Moon not only confirmed that the Earth was in fact round, but that the Moon was a major focus in the heavens and could be relied upon for her cyclical presence.

The Moon's Position and Physical Form

As the Earth's only satellite, the Moon was formed over four billion years ago, and about thirty to fifty million years after the solar system was created.

Rotation

The Moon is in what is called a 'synchronous rotation' with the Earth. In other words, the same side of the Moon is always facing the Earth. That's why we always see the familiar pattern of her lit-up lunar landscape and believe, therefore, that she must have a dark side.

Surface

The surface of the Moon is made up of brighter mountainous regions and darker hollows, which are known as *maria*, Latin for 'seas'. These are not actually seas, but vast impact basins, or craters, filled with rocks. The so-called 'Man in the Moon' is made up of these two types of landscape.

Craters

The many craters which make up the Moon's surface are the result of meteorite crashes. The largest are about 200 kilometres in diameter; the smallest are only about one metre across. They were formed over 3000 million years ago.

Tides

We all know that the rise and fall of the tides on Earth is mostly due to the gravitational influence of the Moon. As the Moon orbits the Earth, she also causes the solid rock surface of the Earth to bulge and then retract: not enough to notice, as it's only by a few centimetres with every tide, but enough to exert an influence on the natural environment and inhabitants of the Earth. Without the changing tides and their vibrational effect on the Earth's surface, there are many species who would not survive, such as Galápagos marine iguanas, African dung beetles and fiddler crabs.

Moving Away

The Moon is moving approximately 3.8 centimetres away from our planet every year. It is estimated that she will continue to do so for around fifty billion years. By then, the Moon will take about forty-seven days to orbit the Earth, instead of the current 27.3 days.

The astronomical calculation for the lunar monthly cycle is measured in what is known as 'sidereal' time. In other words, how long it takes for the Moon to orbit the Earth is measured against the backdrop of the constellations and specific stars. Stars such as Sirius or Aldebaran are known as 'fixed stars' because they appear to never move, unlike the planets of the solar system, which move around the ecliptic (the apparent path of the Sun as it moves through the celestial sphere surrounding the Earth).

Zero Atmosphere

With zero atmosphere, the surface of the Moon is unprotected from cosmic rays, meteorites and solar winds. It has huge temperature variations and no sound. If you were to stand on the Moon (as a few astronauts have witnessed), the sky is always black. Even during the lunar day, when the Sun is shining in the Moon's sky, the sky will never be blue, or light, due to the lack of atmosphere.

The Dark Side of the Moon

Both sides of the Moon get the same amount of sunlight; however, only one face of the Moon is ever seen from Earth. This is because the Moon rotates around its own axis in the same time it takes to orbit the Earth, meaning the same side is always facing the Earth. The side always facing away from Earth has only been seen by the human eye from spacecraft.

However, the Moon's mystique has led to myths, art, songs and other traditions which describe the 'dark side of the Moon' as exactly that, unlit and mysterious. We will explore this later, because everything has a dark side – even the Moon.

Moonquakes

Moonquakes are caused by the gravitational pull of the Earth. Small quakes occur twenty to thirty kilometres below the Moon's surface, causing cracks and faults on the surface. The Apollo seismic team documented twenty-eight moonquakes of this type between 1972 and 1977. Scientists also believe the Moon has a molten core, like the Earth.

Where is She From?

At 3475 kilometres in diameter, the Moon is the fifth-largest natural satellite in our solar system. But how did she get there? One theory is that the Moon was once part of the Earth and that, when a huge meteorite collided with our planet billions of years ago, a chunk broke away to form the Moon. A lingering reminder that she is 'of Earth', too.

Lunar Apogee and Lunar Perigee

The distance between the Moon and the Earth varies because the Earth is not at the centre of the Moon's orbit and the Moon's orbit is not a circle but an 'ellipse' (an elongated oval shape).

The position where the Moon is closest to the Earth is called 'lunar perigee'. The position where the Moon is furthest away is known as 'lunar apogee'. (This point in space will be hugely important in some astrological work, as you will see in Chapter Eleven.)

Various Names for Full Moons

Cultures around the world and throughout time, such as Celtic, Hindu, ancient Chinese and Native American peoples, have given names to each of the Full Moons that occur in their own month. The 'Wolf Moon' is a traditional Native American name for the Full Moon in January. Ancient Celtic peoples often called the April Full Moon the 'Hare Moon'; the hare was a sacred animal associated with springtime and fertility. In Anglo-Saxon folklore, and in Native American traditions, the Full Moon that usually appears in October is known as the 'Hunter's Moon' or 'Blood Moon'. This is preceded by the appearance of the 'Harvest Moon', which is the Full Moon closest to the autumnal equinox.

Black Moon

In Wicca and other magical systems, a 'Black Moon' is said to occur when there are two New Moons in any given calendar month. The second of these New Moons is referred to as the 'Black Moon'.

Although some practitioners say that you shouldn't cast spells during a Black Moon, others believe that the Moon's energy is doubly powerful (as two New Moons in one calendar month are doubly potent and energising), and can attract and intensify spiritual help and guidance. However, if you are looking for Black Moon spells or similar advice on the internet, remember that the term 'Black Moon' is sometimes used just to refer to when the Moon is not visible in the sky, which would include any New Moon phase. For true Black Moon work, always check the New Moon phases in any month in a calendar or ephemeris.

Blue Moon

We've all heard or used the phrase 'once in a blue Moon', and when we say it, it usually refers to something that happens very rarely. In folk magic, Wicca, some astrology and most witchery, a Blue Moon is defined as a second Full Moon occurring in one calendar month, and is considered by practitioners to be a good time to set yourself projects or seek to attain important goals.

Some historical sources maintain that a Blue Moon was originally a term used in farmers' almanacs to indicate the presence of a thirteenth Full Moon in a calendar year. But which Moon is the true Blue Moon is debatable, because it also depends on how many Full Moons there are in each astronomical quarter, e.g. from Winter Solstice to Spring Equinox. Other sources tell us that there is scientific evidence to suggest that, on very rare occasions, the Moon can literally look 'blue'.

Whatever the case, the Blue Moon may simply be a reference to the capricious nature of the Moon herself, who does not much care for the patriarchal calendar month, preferring to follow her own lunar rhythm and cycle.

Super Moon

In modern terminology, a Super Moon is seen when a Full Moon occurs at the same time as the Moon is at her closest point in her orbit to the Earth (lunar perigee, see page 272), so that she looks, quite frankly, huge. During a Super Moon, the Moon can appear up to 14 per cent larger and 30 per cent brighter than a normal Full Moon. However, if the lunar apogee (when the Moon is at her furthest point in her orbit from the Earth) aligns closely to a Full Moon, we see what is known as a 'Micro Moon', which is when she is very far away and much smaller than usual.

Due to an optical illusion, if we see the Full Moon rising just after sunset, or setting just before sunrise, she will be an extraordinary sight, appearing gigantic in comparison with the surrounding landscape. This is because our brain doesn't understand that the sky is a dome shape, and falsely sees anything in the sky near the horizon as much larger than it truly is.

Eclipses

Our sense of fascination, fear and awe when it comes to eclipses dates back to ancient times. Eclipses can only occur when there is a Full Moon (a lunar eclipse) or a New Moon (a solar eclipse).

Lunar eclipse

An eclipse of the Moon occurs when the Earth lies directly between the Sun and the Moon and the Earth casts a shadow on the Moon.

TOTAL LUNAR ECLIPSE

For a total lunar eclipse to happen, all three bodies, Sun, Earth and Moon, must lie in a straight line. This means that the Moon passes through the darkest part of the Earth's shadow, known as the 'umbra'.

Sometimes if a lunar eclipse occurs in October, it is also referred to as a Blood Moon or Hunter's Moon because of the way the Moon appears to turn a deep, coppery red colour depending on the amount of dust in the Earth's atmosphere. The dust blocks out the higher frequency blue light waves, while letting the longer wavelength of red light through.

PARTIAL LUNAR ECLIPSE
In a partial lunar eclipse, a section of the Moon will be covered by the Earth's umbra. Usually the whole upper half of the Moon will be darkened by the shadow.

PENUMBRAL LUNAR ECLIPSE
A penumbral lunar eclipse occurs when the Moon travels only through the outer, fainter part of the Earth's shadow, known as the 'penumbra'. Only a small part of the Moon's surface is in darkness.

Solar eclipse
A solar eclipse occurs when the Moon gets in between the Earth and the Sun, blocking out the Sun. In a total eclipse, the disc of the Sun is fully obscured by the Moon. In partial and annular eclipses, only part of the Sun is obscured.

If the Moon were in a perfectly circular orbit, a little closer to the Earth, and in the same orbital plane, there would be total solar eclipses every New Moon. However, because the Moon's orbit around the Earth is tilted at an angle of more than five degrees to the Earth's orbit around the Sun, its shadow usually misses Earth.

A solar eclipse can only occur when the New Moon is close enough to the ecliptic, which is why it is rarer than a lunar eclipse.

Northern and Southern Hemispheres

The Northern and Southern Hemispheres see the Moon's changing cycle completely differently.

In the Northern Hemisphere, the 'waxing Moon' appears to increase in size and light on the right-hand side of the Moon's orb, while the 'waning Moon' appears to decrease in size and light on the left-hand side. This is because, in the Northern Hemisphere, we look southward to see the path of the Moon or Sun across the sky.

From the Southern Hemisphere, the 'waxing Moon' will appear to increase in size and light on the left-hand side of the Moon's orb, while the 'waning Moon' will appear to decrease in size and light on the right-hand side. This is because, in the Southern Hemisphere, people look northward to see the path of the Moon and Sun across the sky.

The Moon's Influence on Us

Ancient Beliefs

In ancient Greece and Rome, it was believed that any form of 'madness', including epilepsy, was caused by the Moon. Greek philosopher Aristotle and Roman naturalist Pliny the Elder were both convinced that the effects of the Full Moon had a particularly powerful effect on our moods and emotions. The word 'lunacy' derives from the name of the Roman goddess Luna, the divine embodiment of the Moon, so it is hardly surprising we have carried this association with the Moon in our collective unconscious. Pliny suggested that the brain was the 'moistest' organ in the body, and thereby most susceptible to the effects of the Moon, due to her influence on the tides. Pregnant women were also believed to be more likely to give birth on a Full Moon, and any witchcraft performed during Full Moons in ancient Greece was thought to be of a cursing or malevolent nature.

Sleep and Migraines

Our sleep patterns are thought to be affected by the changing 'light' of the Moon. A recent scientific study has found that sleep can be significantly influenced by the lunar phases, with participants in the study experiencing more disruptions in the deepest phase of sleep during a Full Moon.

Don't forget that, about every two hundred days, these regular lunar rhythms are interrupted by another lunar cycle: the one responsible for a Super Moon, when the Moon's elliptical orbit brings it particularly close to the Earth. Intensifying the influence, these Super Moons (and other Full Moons) can disrupt sleep and hormone levels, and therefore trigger headaches and migraines.

It is also thought by some scientists that the Moon has a powerful effect on the regulation of our blood circulation and that we are likely to bleed more if operated on during a Full Moon.

Fertility and Menstruation

There has always been a fascinating connection between the menstrual cycle and the phases of the Moon. It is believed that women are more fertile during a New Moon and studies have revealed that, when women live in close communities with no men (such as a convent), they are more likely to ovulate synchronously with the New Moon.

However, a study by Chinese researchers found that 30 per cent of all the women they monitored ovulated at the Full Moon and not during the New Moon. In some cultures, there is even a name for this phenomenon: the 'White Moon Cycle'. It essentially mirrors the fertility of the Earth itself, which is said to be most fruitful under full moonlight.

Unconscious Selective Recall

When there is a Full Moon and something odd or unexpected happens, we usually notice the presence of the Moon and tell others about it, vividly remembering the date of the event and associating the Full Moon with the strange occurrence. When nothing unexpected or 'different' happens, we don't remember too much about that Full Moon phase at all, unless we are witches, astrologers, spell-casters or stargazers. Yet many mystics and scientists are still convinced that the mystical (or perhaps we could say electromagnetic) influence of the Moon can induce erratic moods and behaviour, powerful emotions, bipolar symptoms (see below), a higher crime rate and an increase in accidents.

Gravity and Electromagnetic Energy

According to some scientific and psychiatric studies, the mood swings of bipolar patients are rhythmic, and these rhythms appear to correlate with certain gravitational cycles of the Moon.

There are some who say, like Pliny, that if the Moon's gravitational force affects open bodies of water, such as the oceans, seas and some lakes, why not the human body and brain, which are composed largely of water?

It is also theorised that electromagnetic energy in our environment may be subtly changing our brain chemistry in ways we do not yet understand. The influence of electromagnetic energy fields is well known and respected in spiritual healing, such as chakra and aura work, reiki and other alternative disciplines. We cannot see this invisible force, but we seem to experience it, so why not the lunar electromagnetic force too?

One scientific study showed that tiny clusters of water molecules in oceanic plant cells are acutely sensitive to the gravitational effects of the Moon on the tides, with more growth during a Waxing Moon, and little to no growth during a Waning Moon. So why not human cells? Given that life is thought to have begun in the oceans, we may have encoded (in our collective psyche) an ability to move with and predict the changing tides. But as this is no longer of any evolutionary purpose to us, instead of moving with the tides, we simply feel the presence of these cycles, still reacting instinctively to the Moon's calling.

*

If you are in tune with nature and the changing lunar cycle, you can use this spiritual or healing energy to make the best of your natural self, too.

Chapter 2

Myth and Legend

The Moon is fickle, and her imagery and traditional associations support this fluctuating energy. When she is a slender, elegant crescent Moon, she is romantic and full of promise; when she is full, she can appear menacing or overpowering; when she disappears from sight, she is a trickster, unreliable and treacherous. Sometimes she is a bringer of light, at others, she darkens the world. As any ancient mariner knows, you can't rely on the moonlight to guide you (as it is so changeable), but you do know that this cycle is constantly repeated.

The paradox of the Moon is that she is reliably unreliable. She has beguiled and bemused many a culture or tradition, leading them to personify her as mostly a goddess (but many times a god), possessed of equally ambiguous attributes or qualities.

Before we unveil the Moon's hidden powers, let's briefly look at her place in myth and legend. Of course, she has always been used for timing events (such as the Chinese New Year), agricultural pursuits (such as the Harvest Moon), and religious festivals including Ramadan and

Easter. Shamans, witches and magicians throughout history have also used the power of the Moon to time events.

In medieval and Renaissance times, magic and spell work depended on the potency of each phase of the Moon to determine what kind of spell should be cast. The Full Moon was used for spells which augmented power, the Waning Moon to vanquish or banish, the Dark of the New Moon to prepare secret potions or poisons, and the Waxing Moon to prepare for the future. For example, in one grimoire (a medieval spell book), a spell to 'heighten the sense' (specifically for the male penis) instructed the user to light a black candle on the night of the Full Moon, tie a red ribbon around the flaccid member and repeat an incantation to a favoured angelic spirit until the said member 'rose' with the culmination of the Full Moon. Whether this 'erection' was maintained indefinitely, or just on the night in question, was not mentioned! Amusement aside, it is upon these traditional grimoire associations with the Moon's cyclical powers that this book is based.

There is enough material on the myths and legends of the Moon to fill an entire book. Below are just a few examples.

Depictions of the Moon

On a wall in the Louvre, Paris, hangs one of the most evocative moonlit paintings that I have ever seen, although the Moon herself is nowhere to be seen. *The Sleep of Endymion*, by eighteenth-century French Romantic painter

Girodet, is startling in its moonlit aura. The young, idealised shepherd, Endymion, is theatrically lit up by an atmospheric moonbeam, which floods through the foliage held back by an amused Zephyr, the god of the west wind.

Although we can't see her, we can feel the presence of the Moon goddess, Selene, inferred only as a shaft of moonlight who comes each night to have her wicked way with the eternally sleeping mortal. The painting is also known as *'Effet de lune'*, meaning 'the Moon's influence', a vivid reminder that the focus of this painting is not so much the slumbering shepherd, but more the Moon's mysterious power to seduce and bewitch even when remaining hidden.

In many artworks, from the ancient Egyptian iconography of the god Thoth, to the romanticised Full Moons seen in Vernet's *Seaport by Moonlight* (1771), Friedrich's *Man and Woman Contemplating the Moon* (c. 1824) and Van Gogh's well-known angst-ridden *Starry Night* (1889), the depiction of the Moon has been both a way to inform us of the time of day and the lunar cycle, but also to convey something mystical, dark and unknown.

Moon Goddesses

The personified Moon has played a key role in many legends and myths from all ancient civilisations, simply because she is always there in the sky in her dance with the Sun god. (For more detail and practical work with Moon goddesses, see Chapter Nine) .

From the earliest accounts of lunar goddesses such as Ishtar, female lunar deities usually appeared as a triad, reflecting three distinct phases of the Moon. For example, in Greek mythology, the dark of the New Moon was associated with sorcery, death, the underworld and the goddess Hecate, who presided over birth and black magic. The elegant crescent Moon was linked with the virginal goddess Persephone, who was abducted by Hades, as well as Artemis, the mistress of wild beasts and hunting. The Full Moon, pregnant with hope, was associated with Demeter, mother of all living things, until upon waning it descended back into the darkness of Hecate's domain.

This reflects the archetypal human experience of the body's own cycle of birth and death, leading to the soul's rebirth. The Moon also presides over the body, the instincts, fertility and the mother, whose nurture brings into being the next 'body'. The Moon's cycles thus reflect not only the human cycle of growth and decay, but also, within a broader context, the universal cycles of growth, decay and regeneration.

Diana

One of the most well-known lunar goddesses is the Roman deity Diana the Huntress. Like her Greek counterpart, Artemis, Diana is a goddess both cruel and compassionate. Goddess of the Moon and companion to beasts, Diana is nocturnal, a huntress and a protector of nature. She has associations with the underworld, and spells are often cast invoking her power when she is part of the Triple Goddess aspect of Diana, Luna and Trivia.

When aligned with Trivia, Diana symbolises the choices we must make as if we are encountering a crossroads in a dark forest lit only by the Full Moon. Without solar light (or conscious awareness), with only the reflective and sometimes illusory aspect of the Moon, can you trust your own instinctive nature?

Luna

The attributes of Roman goddess Luna (Greek counterpart Selene) were a crescent Moon and a two-yoke chariot, or *biga*, drawn by oxen. Roman historians categorised Luna as one of the visible gods, such as Sol, god of the Sun, and she is often depicted driving her chariot alongside his.

Coyolxāuhqui

In Aztec mythology, the Moon goddess Coyolxāuhqui was daughter of the Earth goddess, Cōātlīcue, and the sister of the Sun god, Huitzilopochtli. Coyolxāuhqui had planned to kill her mother, but when Cōātlīcue gave birth to Huitzilopochtli after being touched by a feather, he sprang out of his mother as a fully grown warrior. Realising his sister was about to betray his mother, Huitzilopochtli cut off Coyolxāuhqui's head and threw it into the sky, forming the Moon.

Medicine Woman

The Algonquin people's tale of the Medicine Woman is a parable warning us to 'be careful what you wish for'. The Medicine Woman wanted to know the secret of the universe, and the Great Spirit (the highest power of all spirituality) sent a Manitou (a spirit) to tell her she that she was asking a question to which humans should not know the answer. But the Medicine Woman wouldn't take no for an answer and asked again. The Great Spirit told the Manitou to say that, if she went into exile forever, one day he would reveal all. So, the Medicine Woman moved to the Moon, where she remains to this day. With her corn-meal cooking on the burning fire, she plaits her headband, while her cat combs her hair. When the Great Spirit finally gives her the answer she seeks, the Medicine Woman will finish her headband and eat her cornmeal, the cat will finish combing her hair, and she will return to Earth. But the Great Spirit knows she will never get her answer.

Moon Gods

In many other cultures, the Moon was perceived as a male deity.

Soma

The Hindu god Soma not only embodied the Moon, but also stored there the elixir of immortality that only the gods are permitted to drink. When the Moon waned, it was thought that the gods were drinking all its magical properties. The Moon was also believed to be inhabited by a magical hare and, when hares appeared in the real world, they were thought to be incarnations of Soma.

Anningan

The Inuit people called the Moon Anningan, a god who endlessly chases his sister Malina, the Sun goddess, across the heavens. In his wicked desire for her, he eventually forgets to eat, and grows leaner and leaner, signalled by the Waning crescent Moon. He disappears for three days (the dark of the New Moon) and with renewed energy, finds food quickly until he becomes the healthy Full Moon again. But his sister continually outwits him as he chases her, so he is forever hungry, full, then hungry again.

Folklore and Legends

Here's a brief look at a few folklore legends associated with the Moon.

Werewolves

The earliest references to werewolves are found in accounts of warriors shapeshifting into wolves in battle, related by ancient Greek and Roman writers such as Herodotus, Ovid and Pliny the Elder. The word lycanthropy (the transformation from man to wolf) comes from the Greek *lykos*, meaning 'wolf'. One Greek myth concerns a man named Lycaon, who tried to trick Zeus into eating human flesh and was turned into a wolf as a punishment.

The Old English term 'werewolf', meaning 'man wolf', derives from Norse mythology when it was believed that a Viking could become all-powerful by wearing a wolfskin belt to channel the spirit of a wolf. By the medieval period, the wolf-man phenomenon had taken hold of the popular imagination. Throughout Europe, it was believed anyone could transform into a wolf by sleeping out under a Full Moon.

However, by the fifteenth and sixteenth century CE, during the first witch hunts, the Church decreed that werewolves were heretics who had made a pact with the devil. Many European cultures believed that, if you were bitten by a werewolf, you would become one during the Full Moon. In other legends, the only way to kill a werewolf was with a bullet made of silver. This originates from a real eighteenth-century French hunt for an animal known as the 'Beast of Gévaudan'. The real wolf was eventually shot down by a hunter, who claimed it was his silver bullets that did the trick. (Silver is also the metal of the Moon.)

The Moon Hare or Rabbit

Found mostly in Asian folklore (although also in some Native American and Meso-American mythology) the Moon hare or rabbit is a mythical figure who lives on the Moon and refers to the dark patterns seen on the Moon's surface, more commonly referred to in Western culture as 'the Man in the Moon'.

In Chinese mythology, the hare is portrayed as a companion of the Moon goddess Chang-O, who constantly grinds the elixir of life, while in Japanese and Korean versions, the rabbit makes ingredients for rice cakes. In each case, Moon inhabitants remind us that we must grind and work to succeed, and not try to rise above the Moon's subtle power.

Eclipse Doom and Gloom

Since ancient times, eclipses were feared due to the ominous sight of the Sun or Moon's disappearance in the sky, coupled with the belief that the luminaries were deities who controlled the Earth. In Chinese mythology, eclipses were associated with dragons, and solar eclipses were thought to be caused by a dragon attempting to devour the Sun. Likewise in Egyptian mythology, the serpent Apep was thought to consume the Sun during a solar eclipse. So, it is hardly surprising that our ancient collective psyche has carried on this belief that eclipses are omens of doom and gloom.

By medieval times, an astrologer casting a horoscope might see an eclipse as a sign the king or leader was about to lose power or lose his life, while a more astute, well-paid astrologer might infer that a battle could be won. Eclipses were signs of imminent change: fraught with terror for some, full of potential for others.

One of the earliest recorded eclipses, predicted by Greek philosopher, Thales, who was the first to calculate eclipse phenomena, was the solar eclipse of 28 May 585 BCE. The Greek writer Herodotus recounts that the eclipse was predicted as an omen (whether good or bad is unknown), but its awesome presence brought to a halt a battle in the war between dynasties the Medes and the Lydians, which eventually led to a truce. A less positive omen was in 1133 CE, where Henry I sailed from England to Normandy on the day of a solar eclipse, and astrologers predicted that he would not return. He died in France not long after.

Lunacy

Lunacy derives from the Latin word *luna* and the name of that lovely Roman Moon goddess, Luna. In fact, Hippocrates, the father of modern medicine, wrote in the fifth century BCE that 'one who is seized with terror, fright and madness during the night is being visited by the goddess of the Moon'.

It seems that the Full Moon, since ancient times, has been considered a major influence on so-called 'lunatics'. In medieval England, those on trial for murder could plead for a lesser sentence (thus perhaps escaping the torture rack and being offered instead a quick death) on the grounds of 'lunacy' if the crime occurred under a Full Moon. Right up until the late nineteenth century, psychiatric patients at London's Bethlem Hospital (often called 'Bedlam', which has since come to mean 'uproar and confusion') were chained and flogged to prevent further madness during the Full Moon.

So, we see that the Moon casts over us not just a gentle, productive glow, but also a menacing, confusing one. Yet at the heart of her capricious and ambiguous nature is the positive power she brings to us through her influence in astrology and magic. If you move with the flow of the Moon's energy, and listen to her cycles and rhythms, you will empower yourself not with madness, but with magic.

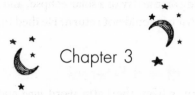

Chapter 3

The Lunar Cycle and Astrological Phases of the Moon

A lunar cycle is the length of time it takes for the Moon to move round the zodiac from New Moon to New Moon, taking, on average, twenty-eight days. Although a calendar month will start on the first of the month, the lunar 'month' doesn't follow this pattern at all, and so will never begin on the same day or at the same time each year.

In astronomical terms, it takes twenty-seven days, seven hours and forty-three minutes for the Moon to complete one full orbit around Earth. This is called a 'sidereal' month, measured by the Moon's position relative to the distant 'fixed' stars.

In the 'Tropical Zodiac' world view as opposed to the 'Sidereal Zodiac' (see box below), it takes the Moon about twenty-nine and a half days to complete one cycle (from New Moon to New Moon), and therefore to complete one full circuit of the zodiac (the imaginary path of the ecliptic). To measure the Moon's movement, we usually take the mean average between the two different zodiac viewpoints (i.e. the Tropical and Sidereal Zodiacs) to come up with a twenty-eight day cycle.

Tropical and Sidereal Zodiacs

The Tropical Zodiac, used by Western astrologers, consists of twelve equal signs of the zodiac of thirty degrees each, making up a 360-degree circle. The zodiac signs don't correspond to the constellations, because the constellations are irregular and no one really knows where one begins and one ends. The Tropical Zodiac begins when the sun enters zero degrees of Aries as defined by the equinoxes and solstices, and therefore is aligned to the seasons.

The Sidereal Zodiac is favoured by Vedic astrologers in India, and although also composed of twelve signs of thirty degrees each, rather than being oriented to the equinoxes and seasons, zero degrees of Aries is oriented to the fixed stars.

Lunar Phases

The lunar phases are determined by the angle and amount of sunlight falling on the Moon, plus the Moon's angle to or distance from the Earth.

For the purpose of this little book, we are going to use the simplest classification of the lunar cycle and divide it into four different phases. I have given you some keywords to get you thinking about what these phases can influence in our lives and how we might use them for spells and rituals.

The Waxing Moon
From the Dark of the New Moon to Full Moon
Keywords: progress, deliberation, seduction, bewitchment, desire, advancement, giving, development.

The Full Moon
Keywords: embracing, enveloping, completion, fulfilment, manifesting, deciding, receiving, concretising.

The Waning Moon
From Full Moon to the Dark of the New Moon
Keywords: unleashing, disentangling, banishing, releasing, dissolving, letting go, dumping.

The Dark of the New Moon
Keywords: re-vision, restoration, acceptance, deliberation, transformation, endings.

The Importance and Use of the Moon in Astrology

The Moon in astrology is a powerful signifier of your needs in your personal horoscope. Chapter Eight is devoted to finding out your Moon sign and working with its energy.

Your Birth Chart

Your birth chart, or horoscope, is a map of the planets in the sky at the moment you were born. Against the imaginary backdrop of the ecliptic (the path of the Sun) and the zodiac belt, the positions of the Sun, the Moon and the planets are calculated, and a map is drawn up by an astrologer. You can have a chart drawn up, or there are many sites on the internet (see page 289) which can instantly calculate your horoscope if you have your time, date and place of birth to hand.

When doing any astrology work with the Moon, it's important to remember this: the Sun represents your ego, your purpose and meaning in life depending on which sign it falls in on your birth chart; and the Moon signifies your moods, feelings, instincts and sense of belonging, according to which sign it is placed in on your birth chart.

When using the power of lunar cycles in any magic work, each sign 'colours' the Moon's influence with a different light as it moves through the zodiac.

Aspects of the Moon

In astrology, there are many other things to consider when interpreting the whole birth chart, such as the aspects, or angles, of your natal Moon in relation to other planets; the phase of the Moon under which you were born; and, of course, the Moon's placement within the zodiac signs and Houses. The Houses are twelve sectors of the horoscope, which represent twelve different areas of your life such as work, love, family, creativity and so on.

The daily motion of the Moon in relation to your own birth chart is also important, as it concerns the influence and aspects of its effects on your natal planets and Moon. There is useful work with the Moon in synastry, where we compare and observe the charts of two individuals, looking at the influence of and aspects between their natal Moons. In synastry, we can also look at the compatibility between person A's planets and person B's Moon, and vice versa.

Dark Side of the Moon

In psychological astrology, the dark side of the Moon reflects unconscious aspects of the human psyche as well as hidden potentials. There is of course, a shadow side to your natal Moon too, but latent or hidden sexual desires and defences are actually revealed through an invisible and lesser known, darker aspect of the Moon's cycle, known as 'Black Moon Lilith' (see Chapter Eleven).

Lunar Nodes

The lunar nodes are two imaginary points where the Moon intersects the apparent path of the Sun around the Earth (the ecliptic). In medieval astrology, they were known as *caput draconis* (head of the dragon) and *cauda draconis* (tail of the dragon). The north node (ascending node) is the dragon's head and the south node (descending node) is the dragon's tail.

In astrology, your natal north node describes the qualities you need to work on to evolve, while your natal south node reveals the qualities you need to consciously abandon or relinquish. The nodes are also sometimes described as representing one's past life (the south node) and one's present and future life (the north node.)

If we are always stuck in the qualities of our south node at the expense of developing our north node, we may find it hard to become successful or content. However, due to the karmic nature of the energy, there will be events and experiences in our lives which will force us to 'get things right' this time round.

Astrology and Eclipses

Put simply, eclipses are no longer to be feared, but more a chance to see your life from a different perspective. The easiest and simplest way to think about modern-day astrological eclipses is this.

A Lunar Eclipse

The present blots out the past; the Earth gets in the way of the Sun's light on the Moon.

In other words: *What do I need to know to help me to live a better life in the future?*

A Solar Eclipse

The past blots out the future; the Moon gets in the way of the Sun.

In other words: *What from the past is stopping me from moving on?*

Working with Eclipses

In magical circles, it is still considered 'unfavourable' to do any spell work during an eclipse, as they have long been associated with negative energy.

When we are working with the Moon, we are working with the 'light' that is cast on to the Moon by the Sun (whether waxing to Full Moon or Full to waning), and also the light hidden at the dark of the New Moon by the alignment of Moon, Earth and Sun. During a lunar eclipse, the light on the Moon is almost completely 'blotted out' by the shadow of the Earth, and therefore becomes redundant. With a solar eclipse, when the Moon gets in the way of the Sun, the Moon occludes the power of the Sun. In magic work, the Sun and Moon derive their power from the quality of light they radiate or reflect. Eclipses are like unexpected trespassers into that light, and therefore carry negative influences.

So when first working with the Moon, use the simple rituals, wishes and enchantments associated with the lunar cycles in the following pages, but always check that you're not working during the time of a lunar or solar eclipse, or your magic may not work out in the way you intended.

Traditional Astrological Phases of the Moon

These are the traditional phases of the Moon used in astrology and magical work. You can, of course, use these as a potent focus for specific work, once you have got used to using the four main lunar phases referred to on page 34.

New Moon – Also called the Dark of the New Moon, this is when the Moon is invisible, due to her proximity to the Sun.

Crescent Moon – This phase is characterised by the first fine sliver of the crescent shape of light at sunset visible to the right if in the Northern Hemisphere, or to the left if in the Southern Hemisphere.

First Quarter Moon – Here we see the Moon as 'half-full' (to the right in the Northern Hemisphere, to the left in the Southern Hemisphere) and still increasing in light.

Gibbous Moon – The Moon is more than half-full but not quite full, and is still increasing in light.

Full Moon – Now the Moon's face is completely lit up. She is considered at her most powerful at this stage, even though she begins to lose light very soon after the culmination.

Disseminating Moon – The Moon is well past her maximum culmination and is losing light.

Third Quarter Moon – The Moon appears half-lit, with light on the left if in the Northern Hemisphere, or on the right if in the Southern Hemisphere. She continues to lose her luminosity.

Balsamic Moon – The Moon has nearly lost all of her light, and appears as a narrow crescent to the left if in the Northern Hemisphere, or to the right if in the Southern Hemisphere, before becoming invisible as the Dark of the New Moon again.

Each of the eight phases above moves through a 45-degree slice of the 360-degree zodiac circle. Each phase lasts for roughly three and half days.

If you were born during a Dark of the New Moon phase, for example, you would have been born within two days before or after the exact degree of the Sun's conjunction with the Moon. Any more than five degrees either side of that, and you would fall into one of the other phases on either side (the Balsamic Moon or the Crescent Moon). See Chapter Eight for more details on which phase of the Moon you were born under, and how knowing your natal Moon phase can help you reach your full potential.

Synodic Cycle

The lunar cycle is also known as the synodic cycle. A synodic cycle refers to the cycle of a planet from one conjunction with the Sun to the next. In medieval magical grimoires, there were usually only two phases that were important, waxing and waning. The Waxing Moon was connected to growth and positive energy, while the Waning Moon was mostly associated with inauspicious, malevolent and negative spell work. Although by the end of the Renaissance, the Waning Moon's power had begun to be harnessed for protective magic too.

The Moon's synodic cycle was tracked from New Moon to New Moon by ancient magicians, astrologers and sorcerers. With its correspondence to our own life cycle, it's easy to see why we associate the different phases of the Moon with different energies. That's what we're going to work with next.

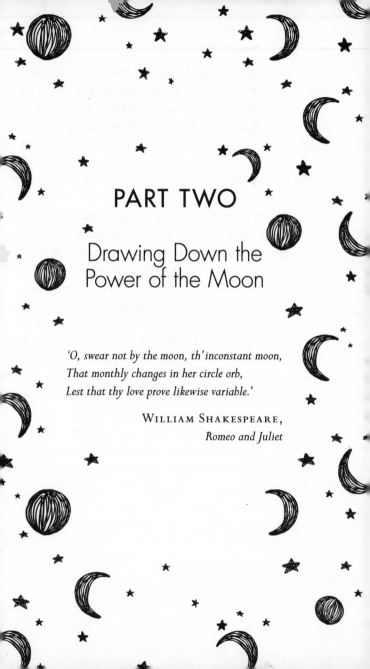

PART TWO

Drawing Down the Power of the Moon

'O, swear not by the moon, th'inconstant moon,
That monthly changes in her circle orb,
Lest that thy love prove likewise variable.'

WILLIAM SHAKESPEARE,
Romeo and Juliet

The Moon gives us the power to understand our emotions, to feel deeply and accept those feelings. She also washes away the things that we find painful. The downside of the Moon is that her power can exaggerate our feelings, remind us of our past troubles, and allow us to become lost in self-doubt and pity. Yet she also has a truly magical ability to fulfil our wishes, dreams and affirmations – if we truly believe in her lunar cycle and work with her changing energy.

The Moon is not kind. She does not wait for us: she retreats and then springs forth, and we either go with her flow or pay the consequences. For the purposes of positive growth and happiness, let's go with her flow.

Chapter 4

Let's Get Practical

Each lunar phase is geared to a specific element of life, achievement, wishing or understanding. We don't have to have a great deal of knowledge on the subject to know that during a waxing phase, things are on the up, and during a waning phase, things are calming down again. During a Full Moon, everything is exaggerated or 'large', the Moon is whole and complete, the light is engulfing, pregnant, about to burst forth. Similarly, many women feel great elation when pregnant or during birth (Waxing Moon to Full Moon) followed by a return to the reality of it all and the knowledge of the dependency of the child upon them (Waning Moon to Dark of the New Moon). Eventually, they restore their spirit, enjoy their children and, like the new crescent Moon, are once again ready for another creative venture, whether of the body or the mind.

Before starting your Moon work, you may want to remind yourself of the four main lunar phases that we will use in this book (see page 35). Once you have these four phases in your mind, and can associate them with the relevant keyword energies, you have the basis for all lunar work.

Preparing for Moon Work

When working with the Moon, the most important thing to know is what stage she is at in her cycle. Unless you are very lucky and have a view of the Moon in a cloudless sky every night, you will have to check this using an ephemeris (a book of planetary positions), a lunar calendar or, probably the easiest option, the internet. Don't forget to check for eclipses, and avoid doing any spells during those dates (see page 39).

Moon Magic

Magic is about making good things happen, either for yourself or for others. This book promotes making things happen mostly for yourself, because if we start to try to engage in or delve into other people's lives, even with the best of intentions, we may not truly know what is right for them, what makes them happy, or what they ideally want or need. That's why all the following spells, enchantments and rituals included in this section are purely for your own peace of mind, your future happiness, or to make love work for you. They are also for the good of the universe and all that's in it.

Working magic with the Moon is about aligning yourself to lunar power, and believing in it, too. In the following pages, we will explore some practical ways to get in tune with the Moon.

Journaling

It is useful to create your own lunar journal by keeping a diary with the dates of each phase, recording your observations and any spells performed. Using this journal to record your work and development through each lunar cycle will help you to understand your own rhythms and connections to the Moon. In the final section of this book, when we look at your natal Moon sign qualities and discover how to work with the phases of the Moon, you can really start to record some fascinating insights into your needs, reactions and relationships with others.

A book, diary, journal or blank sketchbook would work as a lunar journal (the last is a great idea if you want to paint or draw any images that come to you throughout your work).

Unless you find a journal that already contains Moon phases, use your calendar or ephemeris to work through the pages of your journal and mark the date for a 'Dark of the New Moon', then 'Waxing Moon', and so on, leaving two or three pages blank between each one for you to write down information and observations.

You can also record dreams, events and experiences. If you are interested in using tarot, you can do a specific journal reading at each phase to see what the cards reflect during these important phases.

Lunar Correspondences

From ancient Chinese philosophy, Greek magic and Celtic mythology to Wiccan lore, the Moon has long been associated with a range of natural ingredients and attributes that reinforce lunar energy in such a way as to provide you with a pathway for making the kind of magic you want to create. Always keep a selection of the ingredients and attributes below to hand, either in your magic kitchen or your sacred space. Although some of the correspondences listed below are not included in the rituals, you can adapt and mix accordingly, and invent your own recipes for success, too!

Flowers and plants
White rose
Datura innoxia (moonflower)
Ipomoea alba (moonflower)
Night-scented stock
Night phlox
White lily
Night-blooming cereus (queen of the night)
White waterlily
Evening primrose
Jasmine
Tuberose
Anise
Blue lotus

Clary sage
Milk thistle
Hibiscus
Hazel
Blue poppy
Hydrangea
Iris
Passionflower
Bamboo
Hazel
Willow

Herbs, Spices
Gardenia
Ginger
Lavender
Angelica
Rosemary
Sage
Parsley
Mint
Cardamom
Poppy seeds

Essential Oils
Lotus
Jasmine
Evening primrose
Aloe vera
Frankincense

Myrrh
Orris
Almond
Tamarind
Patchouli
Cardamom
Eucalyptus
Sandalwood
Ylang ylang
Juniper
Rosemary
Cedarwood
Peppermint

Colours
Silver
Dark blue
Sky blue
Pale blue
Black
Aquamarine
White
Pearl white

Crystals
Moonstone
Selenite
White quartz
Blue lace agate
Blue tourmaline

Blue agate
Labradorite
Opal
Pearl

Other items
Candles (in a variety of colours for
    various purposes)
A mirror
A white cloth
A small silk or cotton pouch
Paper and pen
Silver rings
Silver coins (see page 55)
Smudging stick
Incense (sandalwood or cedarwood)
A selection of other crystals
Small bottle, jar or phial (for magic potion
    see page 55)
Ribbons in a variety of colours

Your Sacred Space

The first thing you need to do is prepare a 'sacred space'.

A sacred space is simply somewhere special. It should
be somewhere secluded that won't be disturbed by other
people. This is your special space; it's a place where you
and the Moon can connect, interact and feel each other's
power, and where the lovely Moon will bestow you with
her own magic.

Choose a small space: perhaps a window ledge (an

auspicious position that could be exposed to moonlight even on cloudy nights), or a small table, low or high, depending on how you imagine yourself working. Some people prefer a low table so they can sit cross-legged on the floor to focus and meditate during rituals. It's entirely up to you.

I have listed below a range of special reinforcements you can place in your sacred lunar space to amplify and promote both the power of the Moon and also your connection to that power. Keep these enhancements in your sacred space, use as necessary, then replace. As you have seen in the chart of lunar correspondences, there are many herbs, plants, colours, crystals and other objects that can be used in lunar magic. It's entirely up to you which ones you want to use, and it may depend on which you have access to. But here is a basic 'starter kit': one which will quickly align you with lunar energy and encourage positive results in your home and lunar work.

You will need:

A white cloth – to place over the table, altar or window ledge.

A piece of moonstone and a piece of selenite – the most auspicious of lunar crystals. If you can manage to collect a selection of different pieces of crystal, even small pieces, you can create a 'lunar landscape' by adding other lunar crystals, along with herbs, flowers or an image of the Moon to promote positive healing energy.

A mirror – preferably one propped up against a wall, or a hand mirror. Mirrors are reflective, like the Moon.

Four white candles – representing the Four Winds or Directions (north, south, east and west), used to contain and encourage positive energy.

A small jar or bottle of Lunar Magic Potion – Made up of:

> 15ml almond oil
> 2 drops gardenia or evening primrose
>   essential oil
> 1 drop lotus essential oil
> 1 drop jasmine essential oil

Dab this on your body pulse points at the start and end of rituals to enhance natural lunar connection.

A flower or herb associated with the Moon – such as a white rose or lily (see chart on page 50). This can be a fake flower if necessary. Place on your table and refresh as needed.

Your written Lunar Promise – (see page 55).

Four silver rings or coins – the Moon's alchemical signature, to enhance the four main phases of the Moon. Keep these in your sacred place unless you need to use them for anything else, then return them.

RITUAL FOR BLESSING THE HOME AND SACRED SPACE

Once you have your sacred space ready, you will need to bless your home and your sacred space with lunar energy to protect it from negativity. This is best done at the start of a Waxing crescent Moon cycle, when the energy is uplifting and symbolic of fresh starts.

You will need:

> 1 piece of white quartz, selenite or moonstone
> sage smudging stick

1. On an evening during a Waxing Moon, place the crystal on your sacred table, then walk round every part of your home with a lit smudging stick. As you pass through each room, or in each corner, thank the Moon for her gentleness and help in all you do.

2. At each corner or in each new room repeat: 'Thank you, Moon, for the light you shine upon me now, and the help you will give to me in the future. I now clear the air of all past energy to liberate this place for growth and happiness.'

3. Return to the sacred space area, extinguish your smudging stick, and pick up the crystal. Holding the crystal between your hands, repeat the above affirmation.

4. Your sacred space and home are now blessed by the

Moon. You are now ready to move on to the ritual to prepare yourself.

A RITUAL TO PREPARE YOURSELF

First, you need to be completely at ease and ready to welcome the Moon's influence. Secondly, you need to promise that all magic you do is for the good of all. Perform this ritual on an evening during a Waxing Moon.

You will need:

> 2 pieces of white quartz or selenite
> your bottle/phial of Lunar Magic Potion
>   (see page 55)
> 4 white candles
> your journal

1. Place your crystals and journal in front of you on your sacred table.
2. Take the bottle of potion and dab a tiny amount on your wrists, inner elbows and the backs of your knees. This will purify and anoint your body with lunar magic.
3. Next, place the four candles on the altar or table. Position one to the north of you (in front of the propped up mirror), one to the east of you, one to the south and one to the west. (It doesn't matter if these directions are not in line with actual compass

points: it is their position in relation to you which is important.)

4. Light the candles and sit and focus on the candlelight for a few minutes.

5. When you are feeling relaxed and objective, ask yourself the following: What do you really *need* in life, and what do you *want*? Are the answers the same? (If they are completely different, or you don't know what your needs are, it is worth referring to the Moon sign section of this book in Chapter Eight before you begin this lunar work, to help you discover what your needs might be.)

6. Now concentrate on your current intentions. What exactly are they? If you have more than one, or a list, it would be better to write them down in your journal.

7. Next, focus on each intention and, for each one, ask yourself: How much does this matter to me? You can either assign each one a score or a number, or just intuitively know which is the most important for now.

8. Consider how realistic it is to manifest that desire or intention. You can ask yourself questions such as:

   • Am I being realistic?
   • In what time frame am I expecting things to manifest?
   • Can life/love/people live up to my expectations?
   • Can I live up to my expectations of myself?

- Am I aiming too high?
- Do I need to adjust my desire, or look for alternative options?

It is hugely important to consider all of these questions before you do any lunar work, simply because if you don't know and understand what you really want and need, the Moon isn't going to know either.

9. In your journal, write down any answers or further questions so that you can refer to them throughout your lunar work. Blow out the candles and leave the crystals on your sacred table for one lunar cycle to complement all future lunar work.

VISUALISATION EXERCISE FOR DRAWING DOWN THE POWER OF THE MOON

The next step towards drawing down the positive power of the Moon is this visualisation exercise. You can do this on any evening during a Waxing Moon after you have performed the ritual above.

You will need:

2 white candles
a piece of white quartz or selenite
a mirror

1. Sit comfortably in front of your sacred table. Light the candles and hold the crystal in your hand. Close your eyes and imagine the new crescent Moon as a tiny sliver of light glinting in the sky, surrounded by the distant stars. Imagine this crescent shape gradually getting bigger, until you can see the light and shadows of the Moon's surface. Now, half the Moon is cast in light (the First Quarter Moon). As she gains more and more light, she grows bigger, until you are visualising the Full Moon, with her lunar landscape well revealed.

2. Now imagine the Moon gradually losing light and part of her surface darkening. The Waning Moon becomes what is known as the Last Quarter Moon, where only half of her sphere is lit.

3. Slowly, the light continues to diminish, until there is just a tiny sliver of a crescent Moon again, this time on the opposite side. Now imagine the light completely gone. You are in the phase of the Dark of the New Moon, seemingly alone and yet not alone, for the Moon is always there, unlit or not.

4. Imagine now that you are not on the Earth, but beyond the solar system, looking back at the Moon and the Sun. Only the dark side of the Moon is visible, and you cannot see the Sun's reflection upon her or the Earth. This may seem a lonely place, but it is inside you too.

5. Come out of your visualisation. Now gaze at yourself in the mirror and see the light side and

the dark side of the Moon within you. Always carry this image with you, and you will be connected to the Moon's magical powers. Whenever you need to enter into your own 'lunar self' or if you feel that you are not relaxed and ready to perform a spell, repeat this visualisation technique to help you.

YOUR LUNAR PROMISE

Finally, you are going to promise the Moon that you are being true to yourself in all the work you are about to do, that all you do is for the good of the universe as well as yourself as a part of it, and equally that you have trust in the lunar energy to empower you. This means that you need to be sure of 'who you are' and what your intentions are. Once you are sure of a definite intention, you are ready to make a final lunar promise.

You can do this either straight after the visualisation exercise above, or on another evening, as long as it is during the Waxing Moon phase.

You will need:

> your journal and/or paper, pens, collage
>   scraps, etc.
> a mirror
> lipstick or dry wipe marker
> a crystal of your choice

1. Write down these words:

    'I see the Moon, and the Moon sees me,
    Please let the light that shines on me
    Shine on the whole of the Universe too.'

    You can illustrate your message with drawings
    of the Moon, or make up a collage using scrap
    images. Be creative. This is to be kept either as
    a part of your sacred space, or placed in your
    journal to reinforce your dedication.

2. Now repeat the phrase four times as you touch
    each candle (not the flame!).
3. Next, write the words out again on your mirror,
    either with lipstick or a dry wipe marker, and for
    a few minutes reflect on the phrase.
4. In your journal, write: 'All the work I do with
    the Moon is for the good of myself, everyone in
    the universe and those that I love.' Say this aloud
    before every spell you cast.
5. Finally take up a crystal and say:

    'Thank you, Moon, for being with me now and
            for the future.
    Thank you for helping me to manifest all
            intentions and desires, needs and wishes.
            You will empower me with your Light.
    This sacred space is now consecrated. So
            mote it be.'

6. Place the crystal back on the table and blow out the candles.

You are now ready to cast enchantments, make a wish or perform a spell or ritual during the appropriate phase of the Moon.

Working with the Moon

Each time you want to make some Moon magic work for you, first 'know' what it is you are seeking. Focus on that intention, light the candles and face yourself in the mirror. If you like, anoint your wrists with the Lunar Magic Potion (page 55), repeat the Lunar Promise (page 61) along with the appropriate charm, and perform the spell.

But before you do any of the following enchantments, remember again how the phases of the Moon are aligned to specific energies.

The **new crescent Moon** and **Waxing Moon** are the best times for beginning new projects and for spells concerning growth and creativity.

The **Full Moon** is the perfect time for finalising projects and completing spell work. (In Wicca, this is when witches celebrate the 'esbat' in honour of the Triple Moon Goddess.)

The **Waning Moon**, between the Full Moon and the Dark of the New Moon, is the best time for spells concerned with banishment, safety or re-evaluation of projects or ideas.

Finally, the **Dark of the New Moon** is the perfect time to cast spells for regenerating self-belief and releasing old or difficult energy.

Empowerment Rituals for Getting in Touch with the Lunar Cycles

To go with the flow of the Moon's cycles, prepare yourself with a few Moon-friendly exercises to align yourself to working with these four main phases of the Moon.

All of the following rituals can be done either at your altar/sacred space, or, if it's not available because you are on your travels or out of your home, anywhere you feel comfortable. You need to perform these exercises at the appropriate time of the lunar cycle.

WAXING MOON EMPOWERMENT

To begin your work with the Moon's cycles, we're going to start with the early days of the Waxing Moon, when there is a new crescent Moon. There is a sense of renewal and creativity, and an uplift of positive energy in the air. Perform this ritual to align you with this kind of energy, so you will then be ready for the other lunar cycle energies. As you go through the final steps here, don't forget to reflect on what you are feeling and how you are being empowered. This ritual is probably the most important of the four empowerment rituals here, as it is the basis for the rest of the phases to come.

You will need:

five white candles
a large piece of paper and pen

1. Begin by lighting one candle. Relax and visualise yourself being in touch with the Moon's energy.
2. Draw a pentacle on the piece of paper. This is a five-pointed star with a single point facing north (or towards the top of the paper). If you can draw your pentacle in one line without taking your pen off the paper, it will imbue you with magical energy. The pentacle's points represent all four phases of the Moon, plus you. In this pentacle, you are the northern or very top point of the star. The bottom right point is the Waxing Moon, the top right point is the Full Moon, the top left point is the Waning Moon and the Dark of the New Moon is the bottom left point.
3. Draw a circle round the pentacle, so it now appears as what is called a pentagram, a familiar image in Wiccan magic.

4. With the index finger of your writing hand, touch the Waxing Moon point and say:

*'I call you, element of Earth, to bring me
        practical creative guidance.
I call you, element of Air, to help me be touched
        with logic and fresh ideas.
I call you, element of Fire, to help me find
        inspiration and innovation.
I call you, element of Water, to give me
        imagination and self-belief.'*

5. Repeat the same charm for each of the other four points, moving in an anticlockwise direction.
6. Now draw a new crescent Moon in the centre of your pentagram to fix the new Waxing Moon's energy to this place.
7. Gaze for a while at your image, and as you do so feel the power of the four elemental qualities which are enhanced during the Waxing Moon.
8. Light the remaining four candles, one at a time, to 'trigger' the change of elemental energy.

- Light a candle for a sense of practical creativity (Earth energy). As you connect to the energy, say aloud: 'I feel the Earth move within me.'
- Light a candle to invoke a sense of excitement and revitalised spirit (Fire energy). As you connect to the energy, say

aloud: 'I feel the fire of inspiration burn
around and through me.'

- Light a candle for a sense of rational and logical
  foresight (Air energy). As you connect to the
  energy, say aloud: 'I feel my mind filled with
  new ideas and empowered by mental agility.'
- Light a candle to invoke a sense of
  imaginative power (Water energy). As you
  connect to the energy, say aloud: 'I feel my
  soul moved by imagination.'

9. Focus for a while on the pentagram in the candlelight. Then, when you feel calm and complete,
   blow out the candles.

You only have to do this ritual once, and you'll always
feel empowered and ready to work with any spells associated with the Waxing Moon.

FULL MOON EMPOWERMENT

The Full Moon can be a very difficult time for those of us
who are sensitive to the sense of culminating, high-wired
energy, often accompanied by emotional tension or a lack
of control of our feelings. Yet it is also the perfect time
to fulfil a wish, to finalise that deal you had planned two
weeks before, or to cement a relationship. The time of
the Full Moon is, of course, fraught with the problem
of other people's moods and desires and, perhaps more
importantly, how they interact with yours.

To understand this energy and work with it to empower you and keep you on track, whatever other people are saying or doing which may deflect or divert you from your goal, perform this ritual during the evening of the Full Moon.

Once you have learned how to empower yourself in this way, you will find that all spells undertaken during a Full Moon will work for you. You can repeat this ritual every Full Moon, until you are completely confident in your empowerment.

You will need:

> a mirror
> lipstick or a dry wipe marker
> 2 red candles (for self-belief and dedication to
>   your desire)

1. On the evening of a Full Moon, sit before your mirror at your altar or sacred table. Light the two red candles and place them on either side of the mirror.

2. Gaze for a few moments at your reflection in the mirror and focus on how you would like to finalise a plan or solve a relationship issue; perhaps you want to get a commitment from someone, or close a deal. As with all reinforcement rituals, if you align with positive thinking and feeling, you will get positive results. So, during these meditative moments, you will connect with the Moon's

power for motivated strength, emotional open-
ness, and love for the universe.

3. Next, take up the lipstick or marker and write the
   following spell on the mirror:

   'By the fire of passion I will get my way;
   By the red of these flames I will seize the day;
   By the love of myself I will conquer a quest;
   By the Full of the Moon I'll be given my best.'

   The act of writing this is the ritual, but it will also
   bring you closer to your own innate connection
   to the lunar joy, spirit and personal fulfilment
   which is yours by right at the culmination of the
   Full Moon.

4. Repeat the incantation five times, either aloud or
   in your mind, as you face yourself in the mirror.
   No cheating: don't look behind you or at the
   candle flames. Stare into your own eyes to see the
   truth of yourself and the light of the Moon shining
   through you. This ritual will leave you ready for
   Full Moon work.

WANING MOON EMPOWERMENT

The Waning Moon phase is a time when we can feel a
little melancholy, especially if we were born in a Waxing
or Full Moon phase (see Chapter Seven). The sense of a
cycle coming towards its end can be dispiriting and make

us yearn to hide away from the world until this energy has passed. But, like any cycle, we must remember that if the darkness comes, light always follows. So, this phase is an excellent opportunity to prepare for good times ahead; to take a step back, retreat, revise your crazier plans, or come down to earth and see a situation for what it really is. Gone are high-flying ideals, but in comes a realisation of what you've achieved and what can be built in the future.

Although this is a reflective time, it isn't necessarily a static time. During this ritual you will actually be a lot more active than for any of the other lunar phase empowerment rituals. Carry out this ritual only during the waning phase of the Moon.

You will need:

> a crossroads of some kind: this could be an
>> intersection of paths, a set of stairs, a garden gate –
>> anywhere that offers a transition or entrance/exit
>> from one place to another (if you don't have access
>> to such a place, you can draw a crossroads on a
>> piece of paper, or find a map with a crossroads you
>> like the look of, and lay it out on your altar)
> a mirror
> a white candle
> a black candle
> a small bunch of either lavender, angelica or
>> white roses (if you can't get real flowers, use
>> fake ones)
> a black ribbon

1. Once you have located the transitional place, prepare your sacred space. Place the mirror on your altar or sacred table and place the white candle in front of it. Place the black candle on a table behind you. Tie up your bunch of flowers with the black ribbon, take the bouquet with you and head off to your crossroads location. Go to this place during the day, as the final part of the ritual will be done in the evening or at night.

2. When you get to your crossroads, place your small bunch of lunar flowers in a spot that is well hidden from most passers-by. Your aim is for the offering to stay there overnight. (If you are working on a drawing or map instead, simply place the flowers on the point of the crossroads on the map. However, the energy of the Moon will be far more potent if you actually 'do' this physical activity and engage with nature and the elements.)

3. As you place the flowers say: 'Thank you, Luna, for guiding me thus far along the way; I now return what I have taken, but only ask that I can let go of those things which trouble me, and review my desires throughout the lunar cycle.'

4. Now return to your altar empty handed. In the evening, light the white candle, then the black candle. (The white candle represents the future, the black candle the past.)

5. Sit in front of the mirror and gaze into your own eyes. Now close them and be connected to an inner sense of 'letting go' and resolution; of tidying up,

of leaving that beautiful bunch of flowers out there in nowhere land, not knowing if someone will steal it, and whether what you have left behind will still be there for another evening. Instinctively, you will become aware that, if the offering is lost or taken, something else will be found.

6. Relax and feel better for letting go. Blow out the candles, and you will feel empowered by the Waning Moon and ready to work with her releasing energy for any spells to come. Repeat this ritual as needed.

THE DARK OF THE NEW MOON EMPOWERMENT

Many Wicca practitioners don't perform spells or rituals during the Dark of the New Moon, feeling that it is a time for inward reflection and for the final clean up before the dawn of the new Waxing Moon.

However, it is quite appropriate and useful to work with this energy with a selection of charms and rituals where you can truly 'tie up' loose ends, dump emotional baggage, or bring closure to a difficult relationship or other issues that went wrong, so that you're ready to start anew with a clean slate.

To align to this darker, mysterious energy, you are going to perform a visualisation technique and visit the stark lunar landscape itself.

You will need:

a red candle (for self-realisation)
a comfortable chair
a piece of black obsidian, black
    tourmaline or onyx

1. Light the candle on your table or altar. Sit back
    and relax, holding the crystal between the
    palms of your hands, resting gently on your
    knees or table.

2. Close your eyes. If you have never done a visualis-
    ation technique before, simply start by imagining
    something you truly love doing. See it happening
    in your mind, whether it's walking across a moun-
    tain, singing in the rain or laughing with friends.
    Keep focusing on this image for a few minutes to
    put your mind into a kind of open state.

3. Once you are totally relaxed, rotate the crystal
    clockwise three times, and begin the visualisation.

4. Imagine you are walking on the Moon. Visualise
    the craters, dust, endless black skies and glimpses
    of the Earth and the light of the Sun. You are alone;
    there is silence, nothingness. All is empty. You
    place the crystal on the ground and look up to the
    stars. Far away, you see a twinkling light coming
    closer to you.

5. As the light descends to the Moon, the crystal
    begins to dazzle and glow in a burning red flame
    of passion, burning away the dross of the past, and

revitalising the crystal with new energy. The light is absorbed totally by the crystal, and you pick it up again, and immediately feel the heat and power.

6. Say aloud: 'Like the dark of the Moon, I have released all that is done, and am ready to take all that is to come.'

7. Open your eyes and focus for a few minutes on the crystal and the flame of the red candle. The visualisation is over, but it has enabled you to connect the past to the future, and to see that closure means that open doors wait around the corner.

Now that you have completed all the empowerment rituals for the main phases of the Moon, you can turn the pages to see a selection of affirmations, wishes and rituals for each phase of the Moon under a selection of different categories.

Have fun!

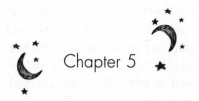

Chapter 5

Lunar Enchantments, Rituals, Wishes and More

The phases of the Moon are dedicated to working with various energies: Waxing Moon to augment, boost or create; Full Moon to complete; Waning Moon to relinquish; Dark of the New Moon to readjust. This chapter is divided into themes to help you decide what you're hoping to achieve first. These themes, such as love, home or career, are filled with spells and wishes which correspond to each phase of the Moon. For example, if you are looking for a love spell to end a relationship, you'll find it in the Romance and Relationships section under Waning Moon. If you wish for lots of money, turn to the section on Abundance in the Waxing Moon section.

Alternatively, if you notice that there is a Full Moon out there tonight, you could simply turn to the different Full Moon sections for each theme, and see if there is a wish or spell you could use impromptu.

This chapter is divided into the following themes:

Romance and Relationships
Career, Success and Goals
Abundance and Prosperity
Emotional Healing and Spiritual Growth
Well-being and the Home

Before you leap into action, it is wise to read the information below on the best way to approach your forthcoming work. In other words, do you know yourself well enough, and do you truly believe in what you're about to perform? If so, is it at the top of your priorities or wish list?

How best to make decisions and work with the lunar cycle comes down as much to practice and dedication as to maintaining a relationship with the Moon. So, if you can, you need to find time every day to align yourself to lunar energy.

Daily Lunar Practice

Apart from keeping an eye on the Moon's phase, either by looking at the sky (if you can) or by checking an ephemeris to work out what stage of her cycle the Moon is in, how else can you 'commune' with the Moon on a daily basis?

Here are some simple daily practices.

1. Believe in the power of the Moon, and remember she is always there for you,

even when you can't actually see her. Keep reminding yourself: 'I see the Moon, and the Moon sees me.'

2. Keep a piece of moonstone, selenite or other lunar crystal with you at all times, or place one on your desk in full view to empower you with lunar energy and to remind you of her power.

3. Keep a lunar calendar diary or make it a daily ritual to write your experiences and feelings in your journal at different phases of the Moon.

4. When you wake in the morning or go to bed at night, thank the Moon for her blessings, or petition your associated Moon goddess for her beneficial energy (see Chapter Nine).

Needs, Wishes and Priorities

What are you currently needing, desiring or thinking about? What are your priorities and intentions? We often think that we know what we want, basing our wishes on other people's lifestyles, media hype, and so on. But wanting isn't the same as needing, and this is where you must be sure of the difference before you call on the Moon. Lunar influence can truly help you to achieve your desires or needs, and these can often manifest when you least expect it, so remember the old witchy warning, 'Be careful what you wish for'.

Discovering What You Need

The words 'want' and 'desire' both mean that there are things lacking in your life. 'Desire' is rooted in ancient Latin and Greek, meaning 'missing the stars to guide you'. So, when you think of desire, think of what is 'missing' in your life. Are those things which are missing of real importance to you?

Perform the following ritual to establish your true desires, preferably during a Waxing Moon phase.

You will need:

   a red candle (for passion and desire)
   a pen and paper, or your journal

1. Light the red candle, relax and think about what 'desire' means to you.
2. Write down a list of the things you want or desire.
3. When you have finished, narrow down the list to one – yes, just one – big desire.
4. Beneath the list, write: 'The most pressing desire right now is: . . . '

Once you have established which desire is the most important to you, your next intention is to find out what you 'need' in life.

Need is very different from desire. Need is a necessity. It's a requirement in your personal life to make you feel content, secure or safe, to give you a sense of belonging, whether to just yourself, or to a bigger clan or family. Needs are what must be met to make us feel comfortable within ourselves, whereas desires are what we yearn for, or *believe* will be great or perfect for us, even though they may not actually provide us with any comfort in reality.

Now take another piece of paper and write down a list of your needs. This can be anything: more money for example, because you are broke (but you must say how much exactly you need, as the Moon doesn't know what 'more' means to you). It might be a greater or more abstract need, such as better health, a more laid-back life-style, or a commitment from a partner.

Again, once you have written down your needs, decide which one is most essential or necessary for you right now and cross off the others.

Finally, write: 'My most essential need right now is: . . .'

Now you have a clear understanding of your desires and needs, you can turn to the appropriate spell or ritual in the following pages to empower you with the Moon's energy, set your intention and look forward to mani-festing your desire or need. Once you voice this to the Moon, she will listen and enrich your life in whatever way she can.

Important Things to Note Before Getting Started

Pick the correct Moon phase
You can flick through the pages to discover which rituals or wishes are best suited to your specific needs and wants, but the most important is using the correct phase of the Moon for the corresponding spell.

Wait for the right moment
This is often where we fall foul of our desires or impulses. For example, we see a ritual for new romance or commitment just as we are in the throes of dating a wonderful new partner, so we perform the spell in the wrong lunar cycle in the hope it will manifest that desire, whatever the phase. But there is a big but.

Lunar warning
Please never do a spell that is described as being dedicated to one phase during another phase, such as performing a Dark of the New Moon spell at the Full Moon, or a Waning spell during a Waxing period. You will simply not get the results you are hoping for, and it may even create disturbing energy around you.

To channel the power of lunar lore, follow the

pathway and trace the Moon's cycles, and you will
discover the happiness you seek.

Wishes and Rituals for Romance and Relationships

Everyone longs for romance: a brighter love affair, a deeper commitment. Love has the mysterious ability to permeate our thoughts, feelings and actions, whether passionate and intense or light, flirtatious and whimsical. The following rituals, wishes and enchantments are performed according to the energy of the Moon's various phases, and are designed to help you achieve your romantic desires and needs.

For the Waxing Moon

These spells for the Waxing Moon relate to the newness of love, such as attracting romance, successful first dates and enhancing all aspects of ourselves to make things work out as we want.

There are also Waxing Moon charms for taking things one step further, perhaps to ensure you can make a commitment, to know there is a 'future' in a romance, or just to confirm your own attraction factor.

In the phase of the Waxing Moon just before the Full Moon, we can develop a romance into something more meaningful, or take more committed relationships one step further. This is also the time to invest your own sense of commitment into a relationship, or to work out what it is you both truly need from one another to make it work.

Ritual for Knowing that What You Need in Love is Often Not What You Desire

There is a big difference between the love we need and the love we desire. This ritual will give you a lunar connection to help you recognise that difference. Before you begin, think about what you want, and what you need. For example, do you want a passionate relationship, filled with romantic escapades? Do you need it? What is necessary in your love life? Loyalty, trust, commitment? Are your needs and wants compatible? If yes, then so much the better; if they seem mutually exclusive, you may have to readjust your expectations of both. Do this ritual during the Crescent Moon phase of the Waxing Moon.

You will need:

> 2 equal lengths of green ribbon and white ribbon
> (each about 60cm/2 feet long)
> a green candle
> a white candle
> a piece of malachite
> a piece of white quartz

1. Pick up the two ribbons together and knot them five times along the length. As you tie each knot, repeat each time: 'I know what I want in love and that is ... ' Say one word to describe what you want.

2. Place the knotted ribbon on your altar or sacred table and form it into a circle. Now light the candles. Put the green candle to the west of the circle, and the white candle to the east.

3. Place the malachite in the centre of the ribbon and repeat five times: 'I know what I need in love, and that is ... ' Say one word to describe what you need.

4. Place the white quartz crystal beside the malachite and say: 'In love I desire [say your word] and in love I need [say your chosen word]. If these two qualities be twined together, bound by heart, mind and soul, then mote it be, and love will come to me this way.'

5. Focus on your desire and your need for a few minutes, then blow out the candles. Pick up the crystals and place them under your pillow until the Full Moon. By then, you will know if your needs are compatible with your desires, and see this come true.

Wish to Attract an Unknown Lover

If you want to attract someone new to you, repeating this little magical wish in any Waxing Moon phase will help you on the way. By the Full Moon, you should see the results you desire.

On any Waxing Moon evening wish:

> *'Dearest Moon, please find love here to stay,*
> *Let him/her find me from today.'*

Focus for a few minutes on the kind of lover you want to attract.

By the Full Moon, someone will be attracted to you, and will make their presence known.

Spell to Enhance Physical Desire

The lunar rulebook states that we should use spells to make our lives happier, and not to influence others; but you can't help hoping that the one you desire will feel the same sort of lust factor as you do.

This spell simply triggers that desire in the other – if, and only if, they have already felt a spark between you! Of course, if they haven't, it won't work, so no harm is done, and you won't be forcing anyone into lusting after you.

Like all other spells in this section, only perform this during a Waxing Moon phase, or it just won't work.

You will need:

> 3 drops of patchouli essential oil
> a bowl of spring water
> a red carnelian, red jasper or garnet pendant

1. Drop the patchouli essential oil into the bowl of water, then, with your elbow resting on the table, hold the pendant between your fingers and thumb over the centre of the water. Focus on the pendant and relax.

2. The pendant should begin to swing like a pendulum, due to the vibrational influence of your hand and arm, and your connection to the lunar energy. Be patient, especially if you have never used a divining pendant before.

3. Once it begins to swing, repeat over and over again: 'By the power of the Moon, this pendant will ignite their passion.'

4. Focus on the one you want to lust after you, and say their name ten times. If you don't know their name, imagine their face for twenty seconds.

5. If the pendant doesn't swing, or it starts then stops suddenly, you will not be able to divert this person's attention. If it swings until you decide to stop it with your other hand, you will have invoked the power of desire into their heart.

WISH FOR NEW ROMANCE

So, you may have attracted someone to you, perhaps through physical chemistry or some other profound connection. But will this turn into a true romance? Or are you just looking for a new romance? Whatever the case, this wish will make romance work its magic.

On the evening of a Waxing crescent Moon, make this wish:

> 'New romance is coming my way,
> With all of my charms, my spirit and soul,
> Dear Moon, bless desire for me now, and for all.'

Focus on your intention for new romance as you repeat your wish.

WISH FOR A SUCCESSFUL FIRST DATE

You're going out on a first date and you want to be sure it will be fun – this simple wish will help promote the happy times.

You will need:

a small handbag mirror
a piece of paper and pen

1. Before your date, take the mirror and point its face upwards towards the sky; whether it's cloudy or not, the power of the Moon is still there!

2. As you do so, say:

'This mirror brings down lunar power,
To bring me joy this evening now.'

3. Put the mirror in your bag and carry it with you on your date to amplify your greatest qualities.

CHARM TO PREVENT NEGATIVE THINKING IN NEW ENCOUNTERS

Some of us overreact or overthink everything when we go on a first date. Even well into the second or third encounter, we start to panic and lose confidence in ourselves (this is often a lunar reaction, according to our Moon sign – see Chapter Eight). So, instead of maintaining our sophisticated, charismatic persona, we might send out negative signals to our admirer, who may in turn take this as a sign we are not interested in them, or that we are just too vulnerable for this relationship to work.

To counteract this little conundrum, do the following if you are worried, feeling vulnerable or doubting yourself on any first date or new romantic encounter – *but only during a Waxing Moon.*

You will need:

a piece of selenite

1. Carry the piece of selenite with you on your date.
2. If you begin to feel overwhelmed with negativity, run to the loo (or if it's possible, discreetly reach into your bag or pocket) and gently rub the selenite between your finger and thumb for a few seconds. It will boost your lunar strength and promote confidence and charisma.

SPELL FOR SELF-BELIEF

If you are often filled with self-doubt and find it hard to attract the kind of attention you want, or you seem to fail to give out great vibes, or you believe yourself not worthy of romantic attention, here's a spell to put you right. It will bring you the empowerment of the Waxing Moon's wisdom and restore self-belief. And if you restore self-belief, you restore love.

You will need:

a sandalwood incense stick
a gold ring (it doesn't have to fit your finger)
a silver ring (as above, it doesn't have to fit you)
a piece of paper and a pen

1. On your altar or sacred table, light the incense and place the two rings side by side, preferably positioning the gold to the west, and the silver to east, to follow the Sun/Moon declination (reverse this if you are in the Southern Hemisphere).

2. On the piece of paper, write:

   'If I restore self-belief, I restore self-love;
   If I restore self-love, I restore the love of others;
   If I restore the love of others, I restore a sense of
   *   belonging;*
   If I restore belonging, I have self-belief.'

3. Take up the two rings one at a time. In turn, rotate each one clockwise between your fingers four times, then anticlockwise four times. As you do so, say: 'I have charisma and self-belief, and the Moon will light my pathway to love.'

4. When you are ready, extinguish your incense and place the rings under your pillow overnight to reinforce the empowerment. Fold up the piece of paper and place it in a secret or cherished place for the rest of this Moon cycle, until you are radiating charisma.

SPELL TO STIR LOVE IN SOMEONE'S HEART

We often go on a string of dates and believe or hope that the other person is feeling the same radiant glow of love as we are. But are they? Are they just players, or are they serious contenders? Do they see any future with us, or not?

To discover the truth, or to stir someone's ardour or passion (without doing them any harm or forcing them) perform this spell during the Waxing Moon phase.

You will need:

a red candle
a white candle
a pink candle
a small bowl of rose water
a silver spoon
5 real rose petals

1. Set up the candles in a triangle shape on your altar or sacred table. Position the red one, representing potent ardour, at the apex of the triangle. Place the white candle at the bottom left point of the triangle to represent your lunar desire, and the pink candle at the bottom right point, to represent your chosen suitor's ideal of love. Make sure you have allowed enough room to place the bowl of rose water in the middle of the candles, and for you to be able to drop petals into the bowl without burning yourself!

2. Place the bowl of water in the middle of the triangle and light the candles.

3. With the silver spoon, gently stir the bowl of water

in an anticlockwise direction and imagine you are stirring love into your chosen suitor's heart.

4. Once the water is spinning around, take one petal at a time and drop it into the water. Say each of the following affirmations as you drop a petal, to charge your suitor with love for you.

- First petal: 'Blessings, oh Moon, please look down on my love and empower them with warmth for me.'
- Second petal: 'Empower them with your love for all.'
- Third petal: 'Empower them with kindness for all.'
- Fourth petal: 'Bring us love for one another.'
- Fifth petal: 'Empower the one I love with equal love for me.'

5. If the water stops spinning before you have finished, take the spoon and gently stir again. When the water finally stops spinning after your last affirmation, the person you love will be as in love with you as you are with them (as long as you believe!).

WISH FOR A COMMITMENT

There's no time like the Waxing Moon to ask her to help you make a commitment.

1. Although there is no guarantee someone else will respond exactly the same way, make it clear you are committed to your promise as you say: 'I wish, dear Moon, to commit myself to the one I love, and they to me. Please let it be.'
2. Write it down in your journal to seal your intention.

By the next Waxing Moon, you will get the results you hope for, as long as you truly believe.

WISHING CHARM FOR FIDELITY

In these days of fast-paced contact via the internet, text messaging and social media, we are spoilt for partnership choice. We can scan dating sites worldwide for the one who might change our life for the better. But the downside is, can we trust them? Are they with someone else already? Are they seeing many different people, or perhaps not really caring about anyone in particular?

If you have fallen for someone already, maybe dated them a few times and are beginning to feel that urge to commit, this wish spell will ensure they are not double-crossing you.

You will need:

a 30 cm (1-foot) long stick, to represent truth (either a bamboo cane or a stick broken off from a tree)

a small bunch of lavender
a small padlock and key

1. This is an outdoor wish, so arrange to be in the countryside (or your back garden) on a day of a Waxing Moon. Take your ingredients with you and find a comfortable place to perform your wish, away from other people and somewhere you can leave your 'ritual' safely overnight.

2. Place the stick firmly in the ground (perhaps hidden among shrubbery or behind a tree) and place the bunch of lavender in front of it. Hold the padlock in your hands and repeat the following wish:

> *'By the power of lavender, my wish will*
> > *come true.*
> *By the power of this stick, its work will be done.*
> *By the power of this lock, my wish will be found.*
> *By the goddess of Moon and the fire of the Sun,*
> *With all that is possible, this wish will be won.'*

3. Take the padlock and lock it around the stick (even if it falls to the ground, it's the action which is significant), and repeat the spell aloud or in your head. Leave the spell there until the next day, whether rain or shine. Your petition to the Moon and her relationship to the Sun at this time of the lunar cycle is all about clinching, locking and setting down your desire for loyalty.

By 'locking in' your loyalty intention, you will know by the Full Moon if your wish will come true.

For the Full Moon

As we have seen, the Full Moon is a time for completion, finalising projects, getting to the point and making clear how we feel, or simply expressing all of our thoughts and needs. Traditionally, the Full Moon has been a potent time for witchcraft and spell casting, simply because she seems to hold such a powerful influence over us. The light is bright yet unreal, and as a reflection of the Sun, her mirroring effect both influences us and mirrors us, too, showing us that both Sun and Moon are at one within us. Another way of putting it is that the solar side of yourself is confronting the lunar side of yourself, and showing you how to embrace them both in readiness for the next stage of your own 'cycle'.

Meanwhile, in the realm of love, Full Moons usually bring great emotions to a head, whether it's all or nothing confrontations or declarations, or sexual reward. The charms here can help you understand that what you wanted two weeks ago is now available to you, or can reinforce those desires to bring them to completion.

PLEDGE WISH

This wish will confirm your good intentions to the one you are hoping to impress, revealing both your commitment and also theirs, if they so desire.

Draw a pentagram on a piece of paper. Write your own name in each of the five star points. In the centre of the pentagram, write your lover's name.

Stand outside under the light of the Full Moon if you can (don't worry if you can't – the Moon will still feel your energy). Hold the paper up towards the Moon and say:

> *'Thank you, goddess of the Moon,*
> *Fulfil my desire and let it be.*
> *Direct his/her love only to me.*
> *This is my wish, so mote it be.'*

Afterwards, write the wish in your journal to seal your intention, and within one lunar cycle you will know if your intended commitment will work.

Spell for Trusting your Intuition

When we question our intuition, it's usually because we are in a vulnerable place, and our confidence has been wobbled by someone else, or what others think of us. This Full Moon spell will restore a true sense of knowing what you really feel about someone.

You will need:

> a red candle (to symbolise potency)
> a piece of lapis lazuli
> a piece of turquoise

a ball of string
a pair of scissors

1. On the evening of the Full Moon, light the red candle and place it on your altar or sacred table with the lapis to the left of the candle, and the turquoise to the right. The lapis lazuli is for your hidden emotional power and the turquoise is for knowledge. Sit quietly before the altar or sacred table.

2. Begin to slowly unravel string from the ball until it is as long as your arm. Cut the string, place the length on the table, and say:

'By the power of a Full Moon night,
Reveal my instinct that is my right.
And as this twine is cut each time,
The luck of Luna will all be mine.'

3. Now take up the scissors and cut the string into seven pieces. After you have cut them, hold them up one at a time and say:

'One for self-love,
Two for togetherness,
Three for more of us,
Four for understanding,
Five for results,
Six for trust,
Seven for completion.'

4. Encircle the candle with each of the seven pieces of string, blow out the candle and leave on your altar or safe place over the Full Moon night.
5. By the morning, your intuition about your lover will be spot on.

A Wish to Keep a Lover from Straying

Sometimes we believe our lover will leave us or be attracted to someone else, either by random fate or through a choice of their own. This wish will activate his or her desire to stay put. Do this only on the actual evening of the Full Moon to show you wish to manifest this desire.

Say:

> 'He/she will not leave nor stray from me.
> This wish will keep him/her close always.'

Write it down in your journal to seal your intention.

Your love will be secure until the next Full Moon, at least.

Spell for Tying the Knot

At the Full Moon, we often feel that we need to 'tie the knot' in our love relationships. It's not so much about making a commitment as it is fulfilling that initial promise. It could be by declaring a marriage or just living together. This charm brings you closer to the fulfilment of that vow. You can do this spell a day before or on the evening of the Full Moon.

You will need:

> 3 white candles
> a mirror
> a 1-metre (3-foot) length of red ribbon or cord
> 5 white roses or rosebuds
> 3 pieces of white quartz

1. Light the candles and place them in a horizontal row on your altar or sacred table, in front of a mirror propped up against the wall.
2. Take up the length of ribbon and make evenly spaced five knots along the length of the ribbon. As you do so, insert each of the rose stems into a knot (or insert them afterwards if that's easier).
3. Lay the ribbon and roses in front of you, and position one piece of white quartz at each end of the ribbon, and the third piece in the middle, above the third rose. As you place the last crystal, say:

> *'With this crystal here today,*
> *We are tied by all to stay.*
> *With ribbon tied and roses fixed,*
> *We'll soon be ever in this mix.'*

4. Blow out the candles and leave your promise of love for one lunar cycle for the magic to work.

REUNION SPELL

Well, we all have past regrets, don't we? You know, 'the one that got away', or that partner we were with for many years who we wish we could turn back time and be with again, or even someone we met in the past who we just can't get off our mind.

This spell works to ensure you will meet up again with this person, whether by chance or intention, and see the truth of that image you have in your mind. A brief reunion is the magic here, not a permanent one – well, not for now, anyway.

Make sure you do this on the evening of a Full Moon to maximise her influence.

You will need:

> a red candle
> a 1-metre (3-foot) length each of black ribbon, white ribbon and red ribbon
> a photo or other image of your intended reunion candidate
> a blue silk scarf or piece of blue paper, large enough to cover the image

1. Sit before your sacred place or altar, light the red candle, then plait the three ribbons. As you do so, say:

   'With this braid I give my troth:
   True to Full Moon, truth and love.'

2. Next, place the photo of your intended candidate under the blue silk scarf or paper. Place the braided ribbons on top.

3. Now make a petition to the Moon. Place your hand over the scarf and say:

   'Once we were at one, in heart and mind.
   Now Moon, take trust and make them mine,
   If only for a moment's worth,
   So I can understand this lover's truth.'

4. Run your finger very quickly through the flame of the candle three times, to confirm your pledge. Then snuff out the candle.

5. Place the braid in your bag or pocket for twenty-four hours, and the one you have concentrated on will be awakened to a meeting with you. When you do meet up with them, take the braid with you to reinforce your ability to see them in their true light, or to see whether you can rekindle the flame, if that is your intention.

The Waning Moon

In Waning Moon work, you are preparing to eliminate that which you no longer want in your life, or to let go of things from the past which have stopped you from moving forward. So, these spells are concerned with banishment, endings and the slowing down of relationships, perhaps to tone down the momentum of a love affair going nowhere, or just to eliminate negativity.

A Wish for Someone to Leave You Alone

Sometimes we have moved on ourselves, and sadly wish the other person could too. This little wish will ensure that, whoever it is who is still hankering after you, will no longer do so by the next Full Moon.

On a Waning Moon evening, light a candle, close your eyes and say: 'I wish for [person's name] to leave me now and forever, and I wish them all the happiness in the universe. Bless you, Moon, for sealing my wish.'

Write this down in your journal to seal your intention.

A Spell for Banishing Relationship Negativity

This ancient spell was once used to ward off evil by medieval sorcerers. It will enable you to get rid of all that is unwanted in your life, to banish negativity around you, and to move forward and manifest your relationship desires in the next lunar cycle to come.

You will need:

a piece of paper and pen
3 black candles
a moonstone or piece of selenite

1. Draw a large triangle with equal sides on your piece of paper, with one point pointing north. Place one candle at each point and light them.
2. In the centre of the triangle, place the moonstone or selenium.
3. Beneath the triangle, write the following:

    'Take three of one and one of three
    To end all of negativity.
    By candles black and moonstone pure
    I leave behind all things unsure.
    With banished darkness, all begone,
    The lunar change brings all things won.'

4. Once you have written the spell, say it aloud, then close your eyes and focus on the crystal for a few moments.
5. Blow out the candles, but leave them and the triangle in place until the new crescent Waxing Moon to restore positive energy.

VISUALISATION TO SLOW DOWN PASSION

You may have just fallen madly in love, or be in a frenzy of loving where you're so dizzy with desire that you can't see the reality of the situation. This spell will bring sanity and restore reason to your reactions and feelings.

You will need:

a handful of lavender flowers
a few drops of lavender essential oil
1 acorn
a piece of rose quartz

1. During the Waning Moon, lay a horizontal line of lavender flowers on your sacred table or altar, and anoint them with a few drops of the essential oil. Take the acorn (to represent grounding and strength) in your left hand and the rose quartz in your right hand.

2. Close your eyes and imagine the scent of the lavender permeating your whole body as you breathe slowly and relax. Imagine how the lavender is filling you with awareness, good sensations and good sense.

3. Now focus your mind on the acorn in your left hand, and how it is a symbol of growth, maturity and slow, sure progress.

4. Next focus on the rose quartz in your right hand, and how it brings peace, harmony and serenity to

any love affair. Consider how it calms the spirit but warms the soul.

5. Finally, open your eyes and thank the Moon for helping you to calm down your passion, to not run before you can walk, and to keep a realistic viewpoint of your love affair. Although it may still feel like a mad fantasy from a romantic movie, as the Moon's light wanes, you will see the relationship in a less subjective light.

A WISH TO END YOUR INFATUATION WITH SOMEONE

To end an infatuation with someone, wish upon a Waning Moon to bring closure to your feelings.

1. Simply repeat this wish and affirmation: 'Dear Moon, thus ends this infatuation; so mote it be, for all this wish is meant to see.'
2. Jot it down in your journal, and you will be free of your infatuation by the Dark of the New Moon.

The Dark of the New Moon

Spells cast during the Dark of the New Moon are usually to finalise affairs, or to make a complete exit from a situation. This is not a time for turning back, but for ending all associations, letting go of memories and pushing the reset button. Here are two spells to do just that.

SPELL FOR LETTING GO OF
EMOTIONAL BAGGAGE

It's not just about ending love affairs. Often, even after
we have declared 'it's over', we find we are still bound by
all that baggage that got dumped in our emotional hall-
ways. This spell throws it out on the street and lets you
breathe again.

You will need:

a hallway or the main entrance to your home
3 pieces of aquamarine
3 pieces of turquoise
a black candle

1.   Do this during the Dark of the New Moon phase.
     In your hallway or entrance, either on a table, a
     ledge or even on the floor, position the three pieces
     of aquamarine in the shape of an equilateral trian-
     gle, and the three pieces of turquoise as another
     triangle, crossing over with the first, to create a
     six-pointed star.
2.   Light the black candle and place it in the middle of
     the star, then repeat the following:

     'To let go of the past and all that is bad,
     Oh Lunar Goddess,
     Empower me with grace and all that is glad.'

3. Close your eyes and imagine the emotional 'baggage' piled up in your entrance. Now open your eyes, and see that there is none there. It has all gone.

4. If you still feel overwhelmed with emotional guilt, angst or regrets, repeat the spell during the next Dark of the New Moon phase. It will work, but it requires belief and faith, like any spell.

ENCHANTMENT TO SAY GOODBYE WITH BLESSING

When a romantic attachment is leaving, perhaps to travel abroad, or to start a new job in a faraway place, you may not know whether there is any future in that relationship. Long-distance love is one of the most testing of all relationships, but if you send your lover off on their journey without conditions, with a genuine detachment from emotional assumptions, you will soon know if it was meant to be or not. This spell will release you from the chains of conditional love.

You will need:

> a blue candle
> a scrap of paper and a pen

1. Light the candle and, for a moment, focus on your lover's image in your mind. Imagine them leaving and you wishing them well without fear, attachment or expectation.

2. Write their name on the scrap of paper, then carefully hold it in the candle flame until their name is burnt away. As you do so, say:

   'From lovers' chain no longer bound,
   You and I, are lost or found,
   By candle blue and words of truth,
   I bless you now with this my oath.'

3. Blow out the candle, and either bury the candle and the ashes of the paper, or cast them into a flowing river, repeating the words above as you do so. By the following Dark of the New Moon, your gift of unconditional love will put this relationship on a better and more accepting level.

Wishes and Rituals for Career and Lifestyle

In Moon magic, the spells for improving your career or achieving lifestyle goals are most auspicious done during a Waxing or Full Moon. However, if you are hoping to end a career that is going nowhere, or have issues around the right kind of lifestyle, or need to overcome your fear of failure in a successful enterprise, there are a selection of enchantments to be performed during the Waning Moon.

For the Waxing Moon

Whenever we need to boost our career or make a lifestyle change, the Waxing Moon provides exactly the right kind of energy.

A Wish for Greater Things

Whether we are at a crossroads, or simply looking to improve our status or ambitions, we all often wish for greater things.

During a Waxing Moon, light a red candle, then write in your journal: 'I wish for Greater Things for myself, and for those I love; to improve and better myself; and to give back the rewards I receive to make the universe and all within it a better place.'

Repeat your wish aloud to voice your intention to the Moon.

Oracle Spell for Career Path Guidance

Choosing a new career or vocation can't be done lightly, but there are times when we reach a crossroads and either have too many choices ahead of us, or simply feel inert and unable to take the plunge: will I regret my choice? How do I know I'm doing the right thing? This simple oracle will guide you towards making the right choice.

You will need:

> a white candle
> seven small tumble stones or crystals, about
>   the same size: one each of red agate, white
>   quartz, aquamarine, onyx, turquoise, blue
>   tourmaline and amber
> a pouch or small bag

1. During the evening of a Waxing Moon, light the candle, place the stones in the bag and shake gently. As you do so, stare into the candle flame, and focus on what it is that makes you happiest or most passionate in your lifestyle or working life. What is it that really matters to you?

2. Next, say to the Moon: 'I give thanks to the lunar energy to now lighten my pathway.'

3. Put your hand inside the pouch and randomly pluck a crystal from the bag. Place it on the table and use the oracle interpretation below for each crystal to guide you in your choice.

    Red agate – a high-powered, well-paid position; being a leader or the boss

    White quartz – a freelancer, a glamorous role or an unpredictable lifestyle

    Aquamarine – a team player with not too much responsibility; scope to be creative

    Onyx – an ambitious lifestyle; traditional values; conventional working day

    Turquoise – an explorer or long-distance traveller; friends or companions are more important

    Blue tourmaline – working with others in a calm, natural or nurturing environment

    Amber – artistic; writing or creative work alone, inspired by the world around you

A Wish for Success

We all want success in our business, career or work-place. This simple wish is for all kinds of success and, as long as you believe in yourself, your wish will come true.

At the beginning of the Waxing phase, say: 'This wish is for success, for more to come in the best possible way. Thank you, dear Moon, for what is to come.'

Repeat again before the Full Moon to boost the imminent fulfilment of your wish.

Repeat this spell every Waxing lunar cycle and you will attract more success.

A Dynamic Business Spell

This is a very quick and easy enchantment to attract business opportunities and dynamic contacts. It should be done during a Waxing Moon phase.

You will need:

> 1 piece of fire agate or ruby
> 1 piece of labradorite
> 1 piece of aventurine

1. To encourage a dynamic business life, place a piece of fire agate or ruby under your pillow or bed.
2. To attract good contacts, place a labradorite

crystal on a window ledge where there is maximum moonlight to enhance your vitality.

3. For vitalising ideas, creative thinking, and brainstorming success, place a piece of aventurine in your office desk, or by your computer.

POTION FOR BUSINESS RESULTS

When attending a crucial meeting or interview, dab a little of this potion on your wrists and inner elbows, and the backs of your knees. This will attract the right kind of response and make sure you win the deal or get the job.

Make this potion during the last few days of the Waxing Moon. It doesn't matter if your meeting is a few days later or a few weeks later; it is the timing of the alchemical mixing of the potion that is important here.

You will need:

a few drops of bergamot essential oil
a few drops of cinnamon essential oil
a few drops of lavender essential oil
a few drops of sandalwood essential oil
a few drops of cedar essential oil
a small bottle, phial or container

1. Add a few drops of each of the essential oils into your bottle or phial. Mix or shake the potion.
2. As you mix the potion, repeat this incantation:

'By the power of the Moon, let this potion prove
Some lavish success and good blessings too.
By the power of the Moon, draw success my way
And the goals I seek will achieve on the day.'

3. Leave the potion overnight in the moonlight, on a window ledge or a discreet place outside: anywhere the Moon might shine, even if it's cloudy.
4. Use the potion as described whenever those life-changing meetings or opportunities arise.

For the Full Moon

Remember, the Full Moon is great for rituals and wishes which are concerned with intention, completion, confirmation and achievement.

AN ENCHANTMENT TO MANIFEST A SUCCESSFUL VENTURE

You may have made plans and organised your affairs; you may have communicated and sorted out the financial logistics or made the right contacts: now you need things to 'happen'. To manifest your career desires or wishes, follow up any initial spell with this Full Moon enchantment.

You will need:

2 red candles
twine, raffia or white ribbon

a bowl of water

a pouch

1. On the night of the Full Moon, bind together the
    two red candles (representing you and the venture)
    with the twine (representing the manifest world)
    and stand them in the bowl of water on your altar
    or sacred table.

2. Light the candles and sit back for a few minutes,
    focusing your mind on manifesting the success you
    are hoping for.

3. Once the candles have started to dribble wax, hold
    them above the bowl and let the wax drip directly
    into the water for about ten drops each.

4. Blow out the candles and, once the wax patterns
    in the water are hardened and cold, carefully lift
    them out. Crumble the wax into the pouch and
    keep it beneath your pillow overnight.

5. Very soon, the goals you intend to manifest
    will appear.

A WISH TO CLOSE A DEAL

The Full Moon is the perfect time to bring a deal to fru-
ition, or commit yourself to a transformation or change
in your pathway.

1. Close your eyes for a few minutes and focus
    on your intention, or the deal that is about to

be signed off. Visualise the outcome in your mind and say aloud your intention to invoke what will happen. Say: 'I wish to bring this deal to closure, dear Moon, now all about me is attained.'

2. Write down your wish in your journal, and by the next Full Moon your commitment or deal will be successfully finalised.

For the Waning Moon

The charms you can perform during this phase of the Moon are concerned with eliminating negativity in your career or working life.

RITUAL TO ENSURE OTHERS DON'T STEAL YOUR THUNDER

Of course, we all want to achieve something, and of course there are many competitors out there who would like to take away what is rightfully ours, or steal our best ideas before we have time to manifest them.

If you know of an individual or business who may be about to do just that, this ritual will put a stop to their game (in a completely harmless way) and give you free rein to negotiate, plan and get to top position.

You will need:

2 acorns

a very small cardboard box
a piece of paper and pen

1. On the paper, write down the following spell:

    *'The lunar power is with me now
    To stop your meddling from this hour.'*

2. Wrap the paper around the acorns (one repre-
    senting the rival, the other representing their
    interference) and place the bundle in the box.
3. During the Waning Moon, bury the box, either in
    your garden or out in the countryside or, if that's
    not possible, push it into a pot of earth. You can
    even fill a paper bag with earth, put the box inside,
    cover it and put it in the bin.

By the New Moon, you will be freed from their envi-
ous rivalry.

WISH TO BANISH INTERVIEW OR
PUBLIC SPEAKING WORRIES

During the Waning Moon, this wish will bring you cour-
age and a motivated sense of self, enabling you to swap
worries and fears of failure for opportunities to be seized.

In your journal, write: 'I banish fears and worries too;
as fears vanish, success is gained.'

Reaffirm your wish by repeating aloud.

Your confidence and self-belief will be restored by the time of the New Moon, and you will succeed at any event or interview.

SPELL TO END A CAREER OR JOB THAT'S GOING NOWHERE

Sometimes we have to reluctantly accept that our chosen pathway may not be the right one for us after all. Faced with this dilemma, it can feel as though we've failed, when in fact we're just acknowledging that we are not 'right for the job'. To let go and move on, perform this spell during a Waning Moon, as close to the Dark of the New Moon as possible.

You will need:

a white candle
a piece of paper and a pen
a big book (not a blank one)

1. Sit before your altar or sacred table, light the candle, then, on the paper, write: 'I am now moving on with no regrets.'
2. Next, pick up the book and flick through the pages. Without looking, place the book back on the table, open to a random page. Close your eyes again and, with one finger, begin to make circles in the air over the open pages. When you feel

compelled to stop, place your finger randomly on the page. Open your eyes and look at where your finger is pointing.

3. On the same piece of paper, write down any words that 'stand out' to you where your finger is pointing, whether it's a whole sentence or just a couple of words.

4. Fold the paper four times and place it in the book at exactly the page it was opened to. Blow out the candle and leave the book in a safe place.

By the next Full Moon, you will have moved on from the past and a new career or venture will be on your mind.

Wishes and Rituals for Abundance and Prosperity

Most of us not only want success in our work or creative talent, but also to achieve prosperity in one way or another. Our idea of abundance, of course, is dependent on how much we already have of something. Although sometimes it's true that 'less is more', the richness we can feel of spirit, soul and also financial wealth, is an aspiration we all often wish to attain.

These rituals and wishes are best cast during the Waxing and Full Moon period, when your intentions are at a peak. I have included a wish for the Waning/Dark of the New Moon to drive away unwanted negativity.

For the Waxing Moon

SPELL FOR LONG-TERM PROSPERITY

Runes are ancient symbols that have a powerful influence in spell work and are known for their mystical connection to the divine. Harnessing the power of both the Moon and the runes will bring you the long-term prosperity you seek.

You will need:

> 7 smooth round pebbles or stones
> a pen, to mark the rune symbols on the stones
> 7 white tealight candles
> a small box with a lid

1. Look up the following rune symbols on the internet and copy each one on to one of the pebbles or stones with your pen.

    Ansuz will attract important influences
    Hagalaz will activate the spell
    Jera will ensure that prosperity comes to you
    Dagaz brings financial helpers or important contacts
    Mannaz is for communicating your needs
    Wunjo ensures that the results of the spell will be positive

Inguz prevents negativity and encourages good fortune

2. Light the seven candles and place them in a circle. Take each stone in your hand, one at a time, and place it beside a candle. As you do so, say:

'Each rune I place for fortune find,
For my own self and others kind,
This symbol brings me wealth indeed,
Each one enough to fuel my needs.
Thank you, Moon, for empowering me
With your blessed light, so mote it be.'

3. Leave your sacred runes and candles in place until the candles have burned down, then put the stones in the box and keep it in a safe place. Within two Full Moons, your prosperity will begin to flourish.

A WISH FOR JUST A LITTLE MORE MONEY

We would all like just a little more money, but you need to make it clear how much. For this wish, during the Waxing Moon period, you will need to write down exactly how much money you would like.

1. In your journal, write: 'Dear Moon, please bring me [x amount of money] by the next New Moon. Thank you for your support and help.'

2. Repeat your wish four times to align to each of the main lunar phases.

As long as you truly believe in receiving this (realistic) amount, you will.

For the Full Moon

ABUNDANT IDEAS CHARM

Of course, having more of something isn't just about having more money. It can also be about an abundance of ideas, practical solutions, rich creative abilities or talents. So, if you're looking to get more skilled, achieve great thoughts or revitalise your creativity after a flat period, this charm will get the dynamic flow of universal energy sparkling through you as it draws down the Full Moon's power.

You will need:

a white candle
a red candle
a gold ring (it can be just coloured gold)
a silver ring (it can be just coloured silver)
a pinch of ground cinnamon
a pinch of chilli powder
a pinch of ground ginger

1. Place the white and red candles side by side on your sacred table or altar. Place the gold ring in front of the white candle and the silver ring in front of the red candle (this will balance the energies of the solar and lunar principles).

2. Light the candles, then sprinkle the spices on to the flames. They may sizzle and burn brighter: all the better if they do.

3. Take the rings and place the gold ring on a finger of your right hand, and the silver ring on a finger of your left hand. (Usually gold/Sun corresponds with the right, while silver/Moon with the left).

4. Now repeat this affirmation: 'With spirit of Moon and Sun, may all my talents and skills be put to use, and my creative ideas be noticed by the universe.'

5. Let the candles burn down for a few minutes while you meditate on your talents. Visualise doing the thing you enjoy most; see yourself receiving a prize or reward for your skill; imagine your creative work on show or being used by those in power or those you long to impress; see the joy on the faces of your friends or family and hear their praise and approval.

6. Blow out the candles and put the rings in a safe place. Soon your creative ideas will be abundant and bring you success.

A Wish for Great Contacts

Whether you want to meet a helpful mentor or a high-powered CEO, this wish will help you encounter the kind of people you are hoping to meet to help you in your career.

1. On the evening of a Full Moon, simply write down a list of the kind of people you are hoping to meet in your journal.
2. Write down and then vocalise your wish: 'I wish and thank you, dear Moon, for bringing these helpful people into my life.'

By the next Full Moon, you will have met those people who can be of help to you.

Ritual to Ensure Success

The archangel Michael was also known as a warrior saint. Defeating all evil, he was said to empower believers with divine protection. When he is petitioned during a Full Moon, this reinforced potent energy will ensure you get to where you truly want to be, with abundant rewards.

You will need:

a bowl of spring water
50ml rose water

10 juniper berries
2 sprigs of lavender
1 sprig of rosemary

1. Place the bowl of water on your altar or sacred table. Add the rose water to the bowl, then gradually drop in the juniper berries, lavender and rosemary as you recite the following incantation:

   'Archangel Michael, send out your strength,
   So that I can attract goodness into my life.
   With this potion stirred once it will be done;
   This potion stirred twice all evil be gone;
   This potion stirred thrice my life be fun;
   This potion stirred last, my success begun.'

2. Stir the potion with the index finger of your writing hand in a clockwise direction four times to seal your petition to the Moon and to Archangel Michael.

By the next Full Moon, you will be on the path to abundant success, or perhaps even already there.

For the Waning Moon

A Wish to Remove Negative Influences on Your Finances

Write this wish in your journal during a Waning Moon phase and you will find that, by the next Waning Moon, all negative influences will be gone.

1. In your journal, write: 'I wish for all negative influences on my finances to be gone, and for all to be positive again. Thank you, dear Moon, for making my wish come true.'
2. As you write the wish, concentrate on anyone or anything that, to you, is a negative influence.

Good Luck Money Spell

Fortuna was the Roman goddess of both good and bad luck, so when you ask for her help alongside the Moon, make sure you are making it clear you want *good* luck to come to you! You can only perform this spell during the Waning Moon or the Dark of the New Moon phases as it uses hidden, secret energy, which mustn't come to light. It will help you to save money and feel richer in wallet and spirit by the next Full Moon.

You will need:

> 3 black candles
> 3 pieces of malachite
> 3 black ribbons

1. During a Waning Moon, light the three candles in a row in front of you on your altar or sacred table. Place the three pieces of malachite one in front of each candle. Now take up the three ribbons and braid them together. As you do so, repeat the following:

   'Goddess of fortune and good luck,
   Let money stay with me this way,
   Without ill intent, for this I pray.'

   Repeat your spell over and over as you braid the ribbons and tie off at each end.

2. Now tie three knots along the length of the braided ribbons. As you tie them, visualise your financial needs being met and your wallet bulging with cash.

3. Place the knotted ribbons under your pillow to invite Fortuna's good financial sense – and maybe even the surprise of more money, into your life.

Wishes and Rituals for Self-empowerment and Emotional Healing

Feeling good about who you are is one of the most positive and healing ways to restore holistic well-being, especially when we can give out good energy and help our friends, family and loved ones. But sometimes we must do ourselves a favour alone, and not feel guilty that we're not helping others out.

These rituals and wishes are most effective during the Waxing and Full Moon phases to enhance your sense of self and empower you with the energy to self-heal. Those for during the Waning or the Dark of the New Moon will give you time to restore yourself and re-emerge with a new lease of life.

For the Waxing Moon

PERFUME FOR PERFECT ATTRACTION

With this magical lunar perfume, you can align to the Waxing Moon energy and amplify your innate ability to shine wherever you go, whether at work, social events or in your love life.

You will need:

a diffuser bracelet or a lava stone in a pouch

3 drops of patchouli essential oil (for a
   sensuous aura)

3 drops of jasmine essential oil (to attract desire)

3 drops of vetiver essential oil (to draw down the
   Moon's energy)

3 drops of lavender essential oil (to clear your
   mind and open communication channels)

1. Before you go out to dazzle, take the bracelet or
   lava stone and slowly drip the essential oils on to
   its surface, in the order given above.

2. As you do so, make an affirmation of your intention to the Waxing Moon. Say: 'With these
   perfumed oils, I anoint both my inner and outer
   beauty to shine out wherever I go tonight. Thank
   you, Moon, for the joy of being myself and for the
   blessing of sparkling charisma.'

3. Wear the bracelet, or carry the stone in a pouch in
   your handbag, to attract positive attention wherever you go.

A WISH TO BOOST YOUR SELF-WORTH

We often feel a lack of self-worth, whether we are feeling
down about ourselves or just having a bad hair day. Making
this simple wish during a Waxing Moon phase will boost
your self-respect and bestow you with loveliness.

You will need:

a red candle

1. Light the red candle. Gaze into the flame for a few minutes and picture yourself alive and vivid, dancing in the flames of positive self-confidence and esteem.
2. Say: 'I wish, dear Moon, for complete self-worth and the power of positive thinking.'
3. Write down your wish in your journal and blow out the candle to send your intention to the Moon. By the next Waxing Moon, your wish will be fulfilled.

A CHARM FOR COMPLETE EMOTIONAL HEALING

During the Waxing Moon phase, use this general elemental charm for cleansing your emotional field and restoring good feelings, especially about yourself.

You will need:

3 white candles (to represent Fire and
    Air energy)
3 pieces of onyx (to remove dark feelings)
3 rosebuds (to promote happy emotions)
a small ceramic bowl filled with spring water (to
    represent Earth and Water energy)

1. At your altar or sacred table, take up each of the candles in turn and say: 'I charge this candle to invite positive emotions into my life.'
2. Place the candles in a row on a table and light them.
3. Now take up each piece of onyx in turn and say: 'I charge this crystal to remove all negative emotion from me.'
4. Place the crystals in front of the candles.
5. Take up each rosebud in turn and say: 'I charge this rosebud to bring me joy.'
6. Place the rosebuds in front of the crystals.
7. Now place the bowl of water in front of the sacred enchantment and place the rosebuds and the crystals into the bowl. Blow out the candles when you've had a few minutes to focus on your feelings.
8. Leave the enchantment in place until the Full Moon, and you will be bestowed with emotional healing.

For the Full Moon

A Spell for Charisma

The word 'charisma' is rooted in an ancient Greek word for a divine gift, and is also the name of one of Aphrodite's lovely attendants, Charis. We all have charisma, but it can sometimes seem as if other people are shining brightly while we are dull and tarnished.

To promote instant charisma and to feel it surging through you, do this charm on the night of the Full Moon to maximise lunar goddess power.

You will need:

a pink candle
a white candle
a black candle
a mirror, on the wall or propped up
5 white roses or gardenias (you can use fake ones
    if necessary)
5 drops of patchouli essential oil

1. At your altar or sacred table, light the three candles and place them in front of your mirror, with the pink candle in the middle, the black candle to the left and the white candle to the right.
2. Arrange the flowers in a circle in front of the candles and drop one drop of the oil on to each flower. As you do so, repeat the following affirmation: 'With this offering to you, oh Moon goddess, your lunar light will shine down on me, and my own inner light will shine out from me; so mote it be.'
3. Now focus on your reflection in the mirror for about five minutes, while imagining how charismatic you are going to be. Think about how you will light up the room when you enter, or how compelling you will be as you walk down the street with a slight smile on your face. This is your

chance to prove how glamorous and magnetic your personality is.

4. Come out of your meditation and put the flowers under your bed (rather than your pillow, so that you don't crush them with the weight of your head!) during the night. In the morning, you will be filled with charisma. If you need to repeat this charm, do so at every Full Moon.

A Wish for the Best Feeling

At the time of the Full Moon, we sometimes perceive people to be more melancholy, or feel our emotions are heightened or negatively exaggerated. And that may be true, but there also grand, super, wondrous feelings that can burst into life at this time, or inspire you to do fabulous things in the weeks to come.

This charm will boost your emotions on to a positive plane, remove any blues and restore feelings that soothe, bring harmony and augment the true kind of love that makes the universe, and our relationships within it, worth living every moment.

You will need:

a red candle

1. On the evening of the Full Moon, sit before your journal, light a red candle and say aloud:

'I am ready to feel my best.
I am completely uplifted by my feelings.
With this wish so pure, I am blessed by the
        Full Moon.'

2. Repeat to reinforce the sense of feeling your best within you, then write in your journal to seal your intention and affirmation to yourself. You will feel truly blessed.

MERCURY'S NEGOTIATION CHARM

This Full Moon spell will help you with all forms of successful negotiation, particularly when you want to reach a compromise or be in harmony with others. The lunar energy will amplify the power of the crystals associated with the planet Mercury's brilliant communication skills.

You will need:

3 pieces of citrine
3 pieces of aquamarine
3 pieces of beryl
a small pouch
a piece of paper and pen

1. On the evening of a Full Moon, put all the crystals in the pouch and place it in the northwest corner

of your home. This will encourage helpful mentors and good contacts into your life.

2. Next, write down the following charm:

   'With Mercury's help and lunar light,
   Thus harmony comes to me this night.
   For negotiations beyond this day,
   All will be set to work this way.'

3. Fold the paper four times and place it under the pouch of crystals. Leave for one lunar cycle to reinforce your intention for harmonious communication.

Ritual for Sharpening Your Mind

As well as empowering ourselves with harmonious goodness, we also need, at times, to improve our brain power, enabling us to use quick wits or to know instantly how to make a choice or decision. This Full Moon ritual will give your mind a clean sweep, leaving you ready for mental or logical action.

You will need:

a black candle
a white candle
a mirror, on the wall or propped up
2 pieces of selenite
2 pieces of fluorite

1. Place the candles in front of your mirror on your sacred table or altar, with the black candle on the left and the white candle on the right. Place one of each type of crystal in front of each candle. Light the candles and gaze into the crystals for a few minutes. See the candlelight reflected in them, as such brilliance will also be reflected in you.

2. Face the mirror, and now gazing at your reflection, repeat the following incantation (if you can't remember the verse, write it out on your mirror first in lipstick or dry wipe pen, so you can read it directly while looking at yourself):

'Mirror, mirror on the wall,
I am the fairest of them all.
Of all mind's wanderings, mine is contained,
It's sharp, it's sleek, its contents reign.
Thank you, Moon, for insights bold,
To know the answer before it's told.'

3. Take up the crystals and, holding them together in your cupped hands, repeat the verse.

4. Replace the crystals on the table. Now make a decision to be logical and focused in every eventuality. Once you have blown out the candles, the empowerment will begin to work its magic.

For the Waning Moon

Talisman for Leaving Home

We all have to leave home in one way or another in our lives, whether for a holiday or for longer travels: to take on a new quest or adventure, grasp a golden opportunity or simply fulfil a need to explore the world before returning to our roots. Whatever the case, to empower yourself with the greatest spirit of adventure and to shake off any feelings of regret or fear, prepare this talisman to take with you whenever you leave home. This is best created during a Waning or Dark of the New Moon phase.

You will need:

> a piece of aventurine
> a piece of turquoise
> a piece of moonstone
> 3 drops of sandalwood essential oil
> 3 drops of cedarwood essential oil
> a small pouch

1. On the evening before you leave your home, place the aventurine in a northwest corner of your home, the turquoise in an east corner and the moonstone in a south corner. Drop a drop of each oil on to each crystal and leave overnight.
2. In the morning, gather the crystals, which will

now be charged by the energy associated with these compass points in Feng Shui, plus the power of the lunar cycle. As you put the crystals into your pouch, kiss each one and say: 'Thank you, Moon, for safe travels, and ensure my home/family will be happy, too.'

3. Take the pouch with you, and you will be protected on your travels wherever you go.

For the Dark of the New Moon

RITUAL FOR YOUR HIDDEN SPIRITUAL SELF

This Dark of the New Moon ritual will help you to understand your deeper self in order to promote spiritual and emotional healing. In other words, it will help you understand how you can connect to the greater spirit or soul of the world, or the flow of energy which permeates and animates all things. To heighten your awareness of this deeper connection to the universe, perform this ritual at every Dark of the New Moon phase. You will need to know your Moon sign and the lunar goddess who rules it (see Chapters Eight and Nine).

You will need:

3 moonstones
a blue candle (representing lunar light)
a small organza (see-through) bag

1. Take the three moonstones and place them in a triangle on a table or on the floor, to invoke the power of the Moon goddess.

2. Place the blue candle in the middle and light it. Now repeat the following affirmation as you gaze into the candle flame: 'I welcome the hidden side of myself, and trust in [the name of the lunar goddess who rules your Moon sign], who reveals all knowledge and truth to me.'

3. Move the candle to one side, and place the three moonstones in the organza bag. Now whisper one secret that you would never tell anyone; repeat it three times. (By telling your secret you are giving up a special part of yourself to the lunar goddess, so that she knows you are true to yourself.)

4. Now take the moonstones out of the bag and say this affirmation: 'My hidden spiritual self is there before me; I only have to look.'

5. Place the moonstones in your sacred space until the next Full Moon, and you will begin to find a deeper spiritual connection within yourself.

Wishes and Spells for Well-being and Home

For many of us our home is our sanctuary: a place where we retreat from the wider world and where our tastes, decorations and possessions reveal another side of us. Yet some of us find that 'home' is out there in the big wide world, and others still find that home isn't a place they feel much affinity with, preferring to travel light and live in a minimalist way.

These spells, wishes and rituals are usually performed in a Waxing Moon phase to boost the protective energy in the home, but there are some that can eliminate bad vibes, or help you to let go of past influences; these are more suited to the Waning Moon. Whatever your home means to you, there is always magic to be made to protect you and your family, and to boost the general well-being of your mind, body, spirit and soul.

For the Waxing Moon

These spells and wishes are to reinforce your energy levels and ensure your home is positive, prosperous and wealthy in spirit and soul.

A RITUAL FOR HOLISTIC WELL-BEING

This ritual can be performed at any time between the new crescent Moon and the Full Moon. As a general ritual, you can repeat it every month to reinforce your own holistic health.

You will need:

> 5 small pieces of mystic topaz (or
>   multicoloured pieces)
> a white candle

a black candle
a gold candle

1. On your altar or sacred table, place the three candles in a line from left to right, white, gold and black, and light them. Then place the five crystals in a line in front of the candles.

2. Pick up one crystal at a time, from left to right, and say for each one:

> 'To my north and best is my holistic health,
> To my south is my fame and fortune's wealth,
> To my west and east is my home and life,
> To my golden star is my well-being placed
> And so, with this ritual, the Moon brings
>   me grace.'

3. Meditate on the flickering candles for a few minutes before snuffing out the flames. Leave everything in place until after the Full Moon, then keep the crystals in a special box or a safe place until you need them again.

A Wish to Energise the Home

This wish will energise your home, remove any unwanted energy and bring you balance and harmony.

You will need:

> a sage smudging stick
> a piece of white quartz or selenite

1. On the evening of a Waxing Moon, walk round your home with a sage smudging stick to cleanse and purify all the environment and remove any negativity.
2. Hold the piece of white quartz or selenite in your hands and wish: 'Blessed Moon, let this home be safe and energised with love and peace, and so too all of nature, with the goodness of the universe.'
3. Place the crystal on your sacred table or altar, and your home will be filled with positive energy.

A RITUAL FOR FAMILY HAPPINESS

It's not just the home environment that needs positive energy, but everyone who lives in the home, too. Whether you are single, or have a family of ten or two, this ritual will ensure that a general aura of happiness prevails.

You will need:

> 3 yellow candles (symbolic of family harmony, communication and vitality)
> a piece of white quartz
> a 1-metre (3-foot) length of white ribbon or cord

1. Place the three candles in a row on your altar or sacred table, and place the crystal and length of ribbon in front of them.
2. Light the candles and reflect on your family. Think of everyone in turn (or if living alone, just yourself) and how you can make positive changes to ensure a happier home.
3. Take up the ribbon and tie five large knots (any kind of knot you like) along the ribbon. As you tie each knot, say the following:

'With this knot, let love be done,
With knot two, let love be true,
With knot three, this family's loved,
With knot four, we'll make a dream
With knot five, this happy place is blessed with
        lunar light and space.'

4. Place the ribbon back on the table and blow out the candles. Take up the crystal and leave it in the most central place in your home, to radiate happiness all around all of you.

For the Waning Moon

A MAGIC SQUARE TO BANISH NEGATIVITY

Just after the Full Moon, use this spell to clear geopathic stress. Geopathic stress is the dross from the environment around us, such as power lines and cables, underground water courses and negative ley lines, light pollution, energy pollution, or even plague pits and burial chambers that may have been in the earth for thousands of years.

This ancient magic square has a secret code that can be read forwards and backwards, and up and down, across the square. Magic squares like this one were once used to ward off evil. Keep it in your home, and it will help bring you all that you want to manifest in your life.

You will need:

a white candle
a piece of paper and pen
a sage smudging stick

1. Light the candle and write down these five magical Latin words as a square on the piece of paper:

S A T O R
A R E P O
T E N E T
O P E R A
R O T A S

2. Repeat them aloud five times, then take up your smudging stick, light it and walk round all areas or rooms of your home, taking the stick with you.

As you trace a huge arc in the air in each room or corner, repeat the five magical words.

3. Once you have done this throughout your home, blow out the candle and the smudging stick. Keep the magic square in a safe place (or frame it and hang it on your wall, or attach it to a mirror or even your fridge), to keep your home safe and cleansed of all negativity.

From Waxing Moon to Full Moon: The Seven Chakra Rituals for Spiritual Health

The seven chakras are epicentres of invisible, spiralling energy around the body, and are considered to be gateways through which universal energy, or *Ch'i*, may permeate our physical self. The focal point of the chakra 'spiral' is thought to be located just below the navel, a spot known as the 'hara'. If the chakras are blocked or unbalanced, you may find that you have negative thoughts or feel physically tired or depressed. When our chakras are in balance, our life, moods and feelings flow more easily, and we can work better with the fluctuating power of the Moon.

These seven rituals are designed to heal and improve all aspects of your spiritual and general well-being. Reducing stress, they will restore your energy levels and bring your chakras into balance and you will feel 'centred' at your 'hara'.

For complete chakra harmony, each ritual is to be performed separately over a series of evenings (not necessarily one evening after the other) starting from the Waxing crescent Moon through to the night of Full Moon.

For example, start with the Root Chakra on the first evening of the Waxing crescent Moon, then perform the Sacral Chakra ritual either the next night, or a few days later, and so on; but make sure you perform the first six rituals during a Waxing Moon period, and the seventh, the Crown Chakra ritual, on the evening of the Full Moon.

Alternatively, if you feel that something is 'missing' or 'lacking' in your chakras' energy circuit, then you can just do the associated ritual on its own, but do it during the Waxing cycle.

The crystals associated with the chakras are important correspondences to keep alongside your other lunar lore ingredients (see page 50), unless already included in other spell work.

Root Chakra – garnet
Sacral Chakra – ruby or red carnelian
Solar Plexus Chakra – yellow topaz or citrine
Heart Chakra – pink and green tourmaline
Throat Chakra – blue sapphire or lapis lazuli
Third Eye Chakra – amethyst
Crown Chakra – white quartz

THE ROOT CHAKRA RITUAL

Located at the base of your spine, this chakra is concerned with your sense of being grounded. This ritual is invoked to energise your sense of security.

You will need:

> 2 red candles
> 1 garnet
> 3 drops of patchouli essential oil

1. On the evening of the new crescent Moon, light the two candles in a north corner of your home and place the garnet in front of them.
2. Anoint the garnet with three drops of patchouli essential oil. Watch the candles flicker and burn for a few minutes, then snuff them out and leave your ritual overnight.
3. The next day, carry the garnet with you for the whole day, to revitalise your inner sense of being grounded.

THE SACRAL CHAKRA RITUAL

Approximately a hand's breadth below the navel, the Sacral Chakra is concerned with your sex drive, creativity and emotional state. This ritual will enhance your ability to flow freely with your emotions, and to feel able to reach out to others, both sexually and creatively.

You will need:

    3 orange candles
    6 drops of sandalwood essential oil
    6 drops of jasmine essential oil
    1 ruby or red carnelian

1.   On the evening of a Waxing Moon, arrange the three candles in a line. Anoint each candle with two drops of each essential oil by rubbing the oil along the length of each candle. Now light the candles.
2.   Take the crystal and hold it between your hands for a few minutes while you imagine yourself filled with passion and sexual desire. Focus on the candle flames, then relax.
3.   Blow out the candles and place the crystal under your pillow for one night only, to reawaken your Sacral Chakra energy.

THE SOLAR PLEXUS CHAKRA RITUAL

Situated between the navel and the breastbone, the third chakra is the seat of personal power. Rather like having your own inner 'sun', it gives you an ego. This ritual will enhance your sense of individuality and willpower.

You will need:

> a yellow candle
> a piece of yellow topaz or citrine
> 2 drops of juniper essential oil
> 2 drops of cardamom essential oil

1. On the evening of a Waxing Moon, light the candle on your sacred table or altar and place your crystal in front of it.
2. Anoint the crystal with two drops of each oil by rubbing the oils around all sides of the crystal with your fingers. Leave the crystal beside the candle and repeat this incantation:

> *'My will is strong, my power is mine,*
> *My character true, my purpose fine.'*

3. Place the crystal in a south corner of your home until the Full Moon to activate your strength of character.

THE HEART CHAKRA RITUAL

Behind the breastbone and in front of the spine, the Heart Chakra vibrates to the colours green and pink, and is the centre of warm, loving feelings. To revitalise true compassion and emotional and spiritual love, perform this ritual on any Waxing Moon day or evening.

You will need:

a pink candle
a green candle
a piece of pink tourmaline
a piece of green tourmaline
2 drops of rose essential oil
2 drops of ylang ylang essential oil

1. On the day or evening of a Waxing Moon, light the candles on your altar or sacred table. Place the piece of pink tourmaline in front of the green candle, and the piece of green tourmaline in front of the pink candle (for total balance).

2. Rub one drop of each of the oils on to the back of each hand, then hold your hands crossed over your chest. Close your eyes and think of all the love in the world emanating through you and from you.

3. Stay in this meditative state for a few minutes, then open your eyes and pick up the two pieces of tourmaline, one in each hand, and feel their vibrational energy moving through you as you hold them for three minutes.

4. Blow out the candles and keep the pieces of tourmaline under your pillow for one night, to enhance chakral love and to attract compassion and warmth into your life.

THE THROAT CHAKRA RITUAL

The Throat Chakra is, of course, located in the lower end of the throat. It is the centre for thought, communication, music, speech and writing.

Do this lunar ritual during the Waxing Moon cycle to enhance all forms of artistic inspiration, not forgetting your communication skills. Anything that needs to be said, will be easily spoken.

You will need:

3 blue candles
a piece of lapis lazuli or blue sapphire
2 drops of peppermint essential oil

1. During the evening of a Waxing Moon, light the candles and arrange them in a line in front of you on your altar or sacred table.
2. Hold the crystal in one hand and, with the other hand, anoint it with two drops of the oil. Place the crystal gently to your throat, and repeat the following chant:

> *'With crystal blue I change this hue*
> *Of words softly spoken,*
> *Thoughts, music unbroken,*
> *Inspiring all that is art within me.'*

3. Place the crystal in front of the candles and leave for at least ten minutes while you focus on the flames. Blow out the candle and place the crystal in an east corner of your home until the Full Moon.

THE THIRD EYE CHAKRA RITUAL

Located in the centre of the brow, the Third Eye Chakra vibrates to the colours indigo and violet, and is concerned with imagination and psychic ability.

Do this ritual as near to the Full Moon as you can, to heighten all psychic ability. You will feel 'in tune' with the universal energy, and everything will feel as if it's meant to be as it is. You will feel able to see the truth of any matter, and understand what people are really thinking or feeling. This will also restore strong imaginative and visualisation powers.

You will need:

3 purple or violet candles
3 small pieces of amethyst
4 drops of frankincense essential oil
a small pouch

1. Light the three candles on your altar or sacred table and place a piece of amethyst in front of each one.
2. With your finger, dab a drop of the oil on to the

middle of your forehead, and hold your finger there while you repeat the following:

'My Third Eye awakes and with it light,
My Third Eye brings me great insight.'

Next dab another drop of oil on to each crystal. Focus on the candle flames for a few minutes and let your intuitive mind open up to the vibrational energy before you.

Put the crystals in the pouch and carry them with you until the New Moon to bring you foresight, self-belief and clarity.

THE CROWN CHAKRA RITUAL

Situated on the top of the head, this is the centre for truth, spirituality and enlightenment. Perform this ritual on the night of the Full Moon to encourage the inward flow of wisdom and to enhance the gift of cosmic consciousness.

You will need:

> a white candle
> a piece of white quartz
> a drop of myrrh essential oil
> a drop of lavender essential oil

1. Light the candle on your altar or sacred table and hold the crystal in your hand.

2. Gaze into the flame for a few moments, then close your eyes. Visualise a shaft of pure light coming down from the heavens to reach your Crown Chakra, then radiating all around you and through you. Imagine the light filling every part of your body from head to toe.

3. Open your eyes and anoint the crystal with a drop of myrrh and a drop of lavender oil. Hold the crystal in front of your eyes and repeat: 'With this crystal I am enlightened beneath the Full Moon tonight, and forever will be blessed with cosmic wisdom.'

4. Keep the crystal under your pillow for the Full Moon night, then put it in a safe place until you intend to boost your Crown Chakra again.

Chapter 6

Wishing on the
Zodiac Moon

We've been using the lunar cycle as a timepiece for work-ing out when to perform certain types of spells and wishes to maximise the best potential for the results we seek. But there are also times of the year when you can incorporate another energy, that of the transit of the Moon as it moves through the 'zodiac', or astrological signs.

Each zodiac sign 'colours' the Moon with its qualities as she moves through it. So, for example, a Leo Moon is dra-matic and motivational and inspires us to move forwards.

It's easy to work out which zodiac sign the Sun is in from looking at the dates given in media horoscope col-umns, but how do we work it out for the Moon? Unless you are an astrology buff, the simplest way is to check an ephemeris or internet site to see which sign the Moon is in on the day you intend to make your wish. But remember, you also need to know which lunar phase the Moon is in. Wishes made with Waxing and Full Moon energies are for positive changes and achieving results. Wishes made on a Waning or Dark of the New Moon phase are for banishing, forgetting or readjusting feelings and emotions.

In this chapter, I have shared which types of wishes and enchantments will best align with lunar energy according to the astrological time of the year. I have added one example wish for each sign to give you an idea.

Moon Wishes Through the Signs

Moon in Aries

When there's a Waxing or Full Moon in Aries, the energy is fiery, uplifting, spirited and go-getting. It's a time for fresh starts, exciting projects, new ideas and a quest for adventure.

Make a wish during an Aries Waxing or Full Moon to:

- Invest in a new project
- Maintain your independent spirit
- Showcase your leadership ability
- Set the standards you require from others
- Maximise a new romance or adventure

Make a wish during an Aries Waning or Dark of the New Moon to:

- Vanquish all self-doubt

- Revise your pipe dreams
- Reflect on your future goals

AN ARIES 'GET IT DONE' FULL MOON WISH

During an Aries Full Moon, we can quickly finalise any wish or desire.

You will need:

> a red candle
> pen and ink (ink is a sign of power)
> a piece of paper

1. On the evening of the Full Moon, light the red candle on your altar or sacred table and write the following spell on the paper using the ink:

   'With this pen I so inscribe
   Desires and wishes as described,
   Bring me, Luna, all that I think
   And secure my future with this ink.'

2. Now write your wish below the spell.
3. Once written, place the candle on top of the paper and focus on your intended wish for a few minutes. Blow out the candle and leave the spell in place overnight for the Aries Full Moon energy to permeate your wish and bring you results.

Moon in Taurus

When there's a Waxing or Full Moon in Taurus, we can tune into our creative skills or common sense. We feel ready for sensual pleasure, love and romance, and invest in financial security.

Make a wish during a Taurus Waxing or Full Moon to:

- Embrace and enhance perfect loving
- Indulge in the pleasures of the flesh
- Finalise your creative ideas
- Reveal your desire to someone
- Receive or make a lucrative offer

Make a wish during a Taurus Waning or Dark of the New Moon to:

- Banish money problems
- Reflect on financial needs
- Restore order to your home life

A Taurus Desire for Love Wish

This wish is for perfect loving. It is best expressed during the Waxing crescent Moon, but can be petitioned right up to the Full Moon if need be.

You will need:

> a piece of white quartz or moonstone
> a mirror

1. Hold the piece of white quartz or moonstone and face yourself in the mirror. As you do so, repeat the following wish:

    'One to seek him/her,
    Two to find him/her,
    Three to bring him/her,
    Four to bind him/her,
    One to two, forever one,
    So with five,
    This wish is done.'

2. Jot this down in your journal to reaffirm your wish to the Moon. Very soon you will have the perfect love you crave.

Moon in Gemini

When there's a Waxing or Full Moon in Gemini, the energy is communicative: we can trade ideas and make contact with others more easily. Use this to deal effectively with others and put forward your best ideas in a determined light.

Make a wish during a Gemini Waxing or Full Moon to:

- Trade your ideas or wares
- Negotiate a deal
- Communicate honestly
- Put an end to negative thoughts
- Make it clear where you stand romantically

Make a wish during a Gemini Waning or Dark of the New Moon to:

- Dump outmoded ideas
- Banish negative people
- Remove negative thoughts

A Gemini Negotiation Wish

This Waxing or Full Moon wish will bring you great new contacts, along with social and romantic benefits.

You will need:

a white candle

1. Light the candle and, with your arm outstretched, hold the candle before you while you concentrate on your affirmation wish: 'I wish that all

negotiations be positive and manifest my intention. Thank you, Moon goddess, for your help.'
2. Blow out the candle and, by the next Full Moon, you will have the results you seek.

Moon in Cancer

Traditionally, the Moon rules Cancer, so during a Cancer Full Moon (usually around the time of the festive winter season in the Northern Hemisphere), we celebrate with family and friends. Cancer is also a sign concerned with belonging, feelings and companionship.

Make a wish during a Cancer Waxing or Full Moon to:

- Bring well-being to the family's future
- Reveal your true feelings
- Pamper yourself and your home
- Show gratitude
- Embrace holistic awareness

Make a wish during a Cancer Waning or Dark of the New Moon to:

- Dump all emotional baggage
- Release yourself from insecurity
- Remove bad feeling from your home

A Cancer Family Happiness Wish

A traditional woven garland of knotted twigs or branches hung in the main entrance to your house will enhance well-being in the home.

You will need:

> 3 × 60-cm (2-foot) lengths of blue coloured twine or ribbon
> a smaller piece of blue ribbon
> a selection of twigs or short branches from apple or fruit trees, hawthorn, hazel, oak, cedar, pine, even driftwood – whatever is available in your area

1. Knot the ends of the three lengths of twine or ribbon together, then make a plait. Shape the plait into a circle and tie the ends together with the smaller piece of ribbon.
2. Repeat this charm:

   'With this family garland true,
   The lunar time will see anew,
   For homely warmth, so loved this place,
   With all our spirits filled with grace.'

3. Now take up your various ingredients and begin to arrange them in your garland until it is filled with vegetation.

4. Hang the garland on the back of your main entrance door for harmonious living.

Moon in Leo

A fiery Waxing or Full Moon invites you to take centre stage and be the star of any show, whether your focus is love, career, empowerment or lifestyle.

Make a wish during a Leo Waxing or Full Moon to:

- Show you mean business
- Complete any creative endeavour
- Prove you have the talent someone is looking for
- Enjoy living life to the full
- Reveal your best ideas

Make a wish during a Leo Waning or Dark of the New Moon to:

- Resist taking control of everyone else's life
- Get rid of rivals
- Redeem yourself when asking for too much

A Leo 'Spirit of Yourself' Wish

If you want to show off your greatest talents and assets, make this wish during a Waxing or Full Moon phase to maintain your individuality and enhance career or personal opportunities.

You will need:

> yourself
> a wide-open place, such as a beautiful natural
>   landscape or a beach (if you do not have access to
>   such a natural environment, you can use an image
>   or video, but the results won't be as potent)

1. Go to the place you have chosen. Stand in the landscape, whether you are in the pouring rain, hot sun or calm weather.
2. Reflect on what would make you happiest in life, and the things about yourself that make you feel like a star. As you do so, watch the sky changing (or the sea's movement, if you are on a beach). Imagine you are the sea or the sky, impressive, and filled with universal life. Remember that you can project that image wherever you go.
3. Once you have experienced this feeling all around you and within you, take time to see this power within your own life. Every time you find yourself in a moment where you need to express yourself or rise above criticism or blame, imagine yourself back in this landscape: at one, centred and filled with Leo's passionate flames.

Moon in Virgo

The Virgo Waxing and Full Moon energy reminds us that we must learn to organise our lives, accept that not everyone is perfect, and compromise.

Make a wish during a Virgo Waxing or Full Moon to:

- Edit, complete or finalise a project
- Organise your kitchen, workplace or home
- Clean up the loose ends of a relationship matter
- Make a plan for long-term success
- Deliver an important message

Make a wish during a Virgo Waning or Dark of the New Moon to:

- Give up trying too hard to impress
- Resolve to declutter your home or office
- Reject unwanted attention

A Virgo Cleansing Knot Wish

Accepting ourselves, faults and all, can be a very hard thing to do. We tend to resist and struggle against the truth with defensive reactions, saying things like: 'It's not me who's to blame, it's you.' This wish ritual performed during a Waning Moon will enable you to accept the bits about yourself you may have denied.

You will need:

2 white candles
a 1-metre (3-foot) long piece of string or cord

1. Light the candles on your altar or sacred table. Relax and tie seven knots, equally spaced out, along the length of string or cord.

2. As you do so, repeat these affirmations at each knot you make.

- First knot: 'I accept who I am, I accept who you are.'
- Second knot: 'There is more in life than worrying about me or you.'
- Third knot: 'Loving and giving, gratitude and belief are the qualities I embrace.'
- Fourth knot: 'The Moon finds me and I give her my light, too.'
- Fifth knot: 'I am blessed by the Moon and Sun on this Waning Moon night.'
- Sixth knot: 'I cleanse myself of all wrong intentions.'
- Seventh knot: 'I am at one with the universe, so mote it be.'

3. You will be cleansed of defensive reactions and feel squeaky clean.

Moon in Libra

This is a romantic yet fair Moon period, when we are reminded of our ideals and illusions. The Waxing or Full Moon phase is a time for new love affairs to reach their peak, but can they be sustained in the coming weeks? The great news is that Libra's airy energy can breathe new life into most relationships.

Make a wish during a Libra Waxing or Full Moon to:

- Heighten romantic desire
- Rationally discuss your feelings
- Stay impartial and objective
- Make a promise
- Put harmonious energy in the home

Make a wish during a Libra Waning or Dark of the New Moon to:

- Redesign your interior decoration
- Reflect on the reality of your relationship
- Drop your expectations of others

A LIBRA MOON BOARD WISH

If we can stay cool, calm and collected during the Waxing Moon phase, we can usually work with this serene energy to our advantage. This wish will bring harmonious living to your home by using a collection of images associated with the style of living you prefer.

You will need:

cut-out images, photos of interiors, colour swatches, scraps of fabric, etc., according to your personal taste

a red candle
a mood board or scrap board (any size you like)
glue or tape

1. On the evening of a Waxing Moon, assemble your pictures on your altar or sacred table and light the red candle.
2. Begin to create a collage, arranging the pictures and swatches on the mood board. Work for as long as it takes you to complete the board just as you like it.
3. When you are happy with it, repeat this affirmation: 'By my design, harmony comes to this house; and with the Moon, I find harmony in all I do.'
4. Leave your mood board in a place where you can view it each day for one lunar cycle and look forward to creating harmony in the home.

Moon in Scorpio

The Full Moon in Scorpio was once considered ominous, due to Scorpio's association with all things dark, intense and bitter. During a Waxing or Full Moon in Scorpio, you can be assured of intensifying any plans or projects, relationships or affairs.

Make a wish during a Scorpio Waxing or Full Moon to:

- Reveal your deepest feelings or desires
- Completely transform a relationship for the better
- Discover a secret

- Intensify passion
- Rise like a phoenix from negativity

Make a wish during a Scorpio Waning or Dark of the New Moon to:

- Forgive and forget a betrayal
- Take revenge (in the nicest possible way!)
- Banish ill feelings forever

A SCORPIO PASSION WISH

Do this wishing ritual during a Scorpio Waxing or Full Moon to attract passion into your life, in whatever form you so desire.

You will need:

a luxury indulgence (see below)
lots of red candles

1. Begin by allowing yourself a luxury indulgence: buy yourself a delicious box of wicked dark chocolate, pour yourself champagne to drink in the bath, enjoy a sexy romp with your partner, or splash out on a guilty pleasure.
2. The wish is simple. Surround yourself by red candles and enjoy the kind of pleasure you are often tempted to experience, but rarely allow yourself.

3. As you experience the joy of your indulgence, begin to reflect on what passion means to you. Is it a feeling of intense desire or love, or a physical pleasure?
4. Whatever the case, wish for more of the same, and you will soon have it.

Moon in Sagittarius

This spirited Moon exposes us to the extremes of other people's energy, whether that is exciting, wild and free-spirited, or tactless and uninhibited. We may feel this dichotomy within ourselves, too.

Make a wish during a Sagittarius Waxing or Full Moon to:

- Take a calculated risk
- Confirm your independent spirit
- Do something you have never dared to do before
- Get more involved in a romantic affair
- Complete an unprecedented project

Make a wish during a Sagittarius Waning or Dark of the New Moon to:

- Stop thinking about an old flame
- Remember you are only human and not divine
- Revise future projects and plans

A SAGITTARIUS FREE SPIRIT WISH

This Waxing or Full Moon wish enhances your free spirit and autonomy, setting you up for a new cycle of self-belief and revitalised motivation.

You will need:

2 white candles or 2 pieces of selenite
a mirror propped against a wall

1. On the evening of a Waxing or Full Moon evening, sit before the mirror and gaze for a while at your reflection. Notice your hair, eyes and complexion. Just notice yourself: don't judge, comment or find fault. You are as you are; this is your chance to learn self-acceptance, if you haven't already.
2. Take up the candles or pieces of selenite, one in each hand, and point them towards your reflection.
3. Now close your eyes and repeat aloud or in your mind: 'I wish to know the way forward; I wish to revitalise my will, my independence, my confidence, my peace of mind. Thank you, Moon, for blessing me so.' By the next Full Moon phase you will feel re-animated and self-reliant.

Moon in Capricorn

Earthy and conventional, Capricorn lunar energy gives us all a chance to be down to earth and constructive about our lifestyle needs. This is an auspicious time for controlling your desires or losing your inhibitions.

Make a wish during a Capricorn Waxing or Full Moon to:

- Put an end to an infatuation
- Construct your future career plan
- Become financially savvy
- Sign, seal or deliver a deal

Make a wish during a Capricorn Waning or Dark of the New Moon to:

- Reorganise your home or office
- Clear debts (or a feeling of indebtedness)
- Get realistic about your skill or talents

A CAPRICORN MONEY WISH

Use the potency of the ambitious Capricorn Moon to wish for an amount of money that you are hoping to earn, win or acquire by some legal means. Don't be greedy – and be realistic. Don't just ask for 'more money' because the universe and the Moon don't know what 'more' means in relation to you.

You will need:

a black candle
10 coins of any denomination

1. On the evening of a Waxing or Full Moon, light the candle and place the handful of money on your sacred table or altar.
2. Kindly ask the Moon for how much you want: 'Dearest Moon, fulfil my wish for [say the amount] as soon as is earthly possible.'
3. Sit and meditate on this amount for a few minutes. Visualise the amount you have asked for in front of you, whether it's a stack or a bundle of notes, a safe full of bullion, or just enough cash to keep the wolves from the door.
4. Next, pick up the coins and find a corner of the room to scatter them where they won't be in the way or get removed, for example, under a rug, beneath a desk or behind a cupboard.
5. As you scatter the coins, repeat five times: 'Scatter money on the floor, watch it come in through the door. I wish only for what is more to me.'
6. Finally blow out the candle, and soon the amount you have wished for will appear.

Moon in Aquarius

Aquarius Moon energy is unpredictable and eccentric, and brings unusual offers, people and ideas into our world. We may feel more logical and less intuitive, yet it's a time for innovation and creative guile.

Make a wish during an Aquarius Waxing or Full Moon to:

- Successfully put forward your craziest ideas to someone important
- Do something exciting that you wouldn't normally do
- Get in touch with beneficial contacts
- Make an unusual request
- Help with a global or nature project

Make a wish during an Aquarius Waning or Dark of the New Moon to:

- Reconsider a radical diet or exercise plan
- Give up meaningless beliefs
- Drop so-called pals who are not true friends

AN AQUARIUS 'EUREKA!' WISH

If you're searching for bright ideas or just need to be inspired by a sudden flash of universal light, this lunar wish, made during the Waxing or Full Moon phase, will bring you the insight you are searching for.

You will need:

a white candle

1. To invoke your desire to the Moon, light a white candle on your sacred table or altar. Repeat the following, then write it in your journal:

   'Lunar light, bring me tonight,
   The power of greater insight,
   This wish be seen,
   Inspired, serene,
   And filled with all that's right.'

2. Blow out the candle and, by the next Waxing Moon, that eureka moment will come to you.

Moon in Pisces

The Pisces Moon enhances spiritual energy, often making us feel strangely intuitive or psychic. Love becomes a mystical or unworldly experience and we become more aware of our connection to nature and the universe.

Make a wish during a Pisces Waxing or Full Moon to:

- Learn to work with crystals
- Tell someone how you truly feel
- Listen to your intuition
- Trust in your beliefs

• Start chakra or other spiritual healing work

Make a wish during a Pisces Waning or Dark of the New Moon to:

• End feelings of sadness or self-pity
• Put closure on a difficult relationship
• Revive your self-belief

A PISCES SPIRITUAL HEALING WISH

During the Waxing or Full Moon, make this wish to let the light of the universe shine through you and leave you feeling blessed by lunar energy.

1. Place your hand on your Crown Chakra (the top of your head) and say: 'With the light of myself, the Moon is shining her light through me now.'
2. Next, place your hand to your Third Eye Chakra and say: 'By the light of the Full Moon, I am blessed and cleansed.'
3. Finally, place your hand to your 'hara' (the centre of your chakra energy, located a couple of inches below your navel) and say: 'Thank you, Moon, for bringing me the light of All, to see my way and be healed.'

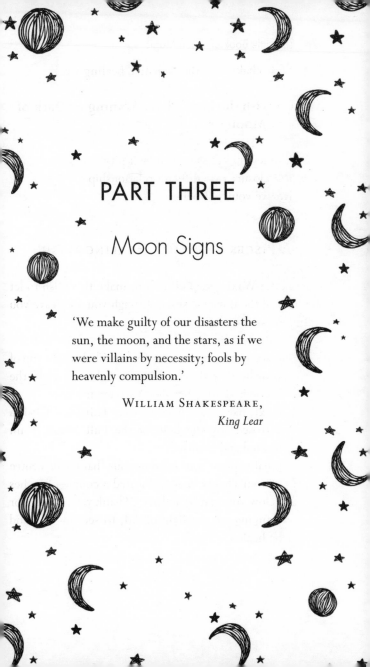

PART THREE

Moon Signs

'We make guilty of our disasters the
sun, the moon, and the stars, as if we
were villains by necessity; fools by
heavenly compulsion.'

WILLIAM SHAKESPEARE,
King Lear

In contemporary Western astrology, when we are talking about our horoscope or birth chart, the Sun represents our goals, purpose and meaning in life, while the Moon signifies our needs, feelings, reactions and comfort zones, as well as our image of 'mother'.

You may well know that Venus is known as the 'planet of love', and its position in our chart describes how we connect to and find pleasure with lovers or potential partners. In combination with Mars, it also describes the romance we feel, or the sexual spark or affinity that makes us compatible with someone. In terms of the astrological Venus and Mars, we may talk about what turns us on, or what we love about someone else; but it is the Moon which informs us of what sort of *comfort* we require in a relationship, and *what we need to feel content*.

Once you have discovered where the Moon was in your chart at the time of your birth, you can use this knowledge to understand both your own and your partner's comfort zones and emotional needs, as well as your sense of belonging and family, and what you both need to feel at home in a love relationship.

Chapter 7

The Moon and Your Horoscope

There are many differences between the Sun and the Moon in astrology. The Sun represents what you are in the process of becoming and the spirit of self within you. It is your future potential (even if you don't know it), and it could be articulated as 'I am', 'I want', or 'I want to be'. For instance, this inner spirit might say, 'I want to shine in this field of work,' or, 'Here, in this love relationship, is how I want to be individual or identified.' In your birth chart or horoscope, it is the Sun that describes your sense of being 'centred', whether that's self-centred (too much ego) or self-conscious (too little ego).

While the Sun sign describes your solar destiny, and the way you discover your 'solar light within', it doesn't exactly happen overnight. Ironically, we often live most of our lives through our lunar selves, which can be clouded by psychological hang-ups.

The good news, however, is that the Moon is your 'natural self': it comes easy, you own these qualities and don't have to look for them through external means, as with Sun sign expression. You may have to wait a long time before you discover your vocational destiny, but the Moon is your instinctive, reactionary and bodily self; it feels natural, even if it's painful. The Moon in our natal chart reveals how comfortable we feel in the external world, and how we react to events, experiences and people.

So in a relationship, the Moon asks you to think: 'What is it about me and what is it about that person that makes me feel comfortable?', 'Do we have the same emotional needs?', or, perhaps more profoundly, 'OK, our needs are not the same, so how do we accept and understand one another?'

The Reflective Moon

Whether the physical Moon has a literal effect on us or not (see page 18), in astrology it is easier to talk about her influence in two ways. First, as a symbolic or mirroring process – the characteristics or personality traits that the Moon describes for each sign she is in (not forgetting aspects from other planets and house placement) – and secondly, the influence of the phases and transits of the Moon through our chart in relation to our natal Moon.

Whether or not the Moon literally *makes* us feel things is an ongoing debate. For example, a client may ask, 'What does it mean when my Moon is in Sagittarius?' As an astrologer, I would probably reply, 'It means that you're restless and feel you need a lot of space, and would feel comfortable with change – but the Moon isn't *making* you feel like that; she just reflects this state within you.'

As the old saying goes, 'As above, so below.' This echoes the reflective power of the Moon. However, there are some astrologers who believe that the daily motion and cycles of the Moon do indeed have a direct physical effect on us, depending on the placement of the Moon when we were born.

Mother

In astro-psychological terms, the Moon also represents our image of the mother: our mothering ability, whether male or female, and also our attachment to our own mother.

This attachment to the mother or the womb reveals the most fragile, vulnerable part of ourselves. Once detached from that umbilical cord, we attach ourselves to 'comfortable' habits, which will sustain us in the way our mother did, whether we were nurtured by a loving mother, a fearsome one, a weak one, or one who just didn't care. The Moon, then, also represents what is reliably known.

Nurture and Needs

For bad or good, the Moon signifies that which is instinctively reliable in our life, and how we go about sustaining or nurturing others. This is a powerful factor in all our close relationships, because it tells you what you need in a love relationship to feel safe, to feel that you belong, and also how you react to the relationship and how it flows. Most importantly, if your needs are being met, can you also accept someone else's needs, which may be very different to your own?

Nature

The Moon in astrology also reflects our bodies: the way we perceive that natural part of ourselves, the flesh and blood of which we are born, and which we must bear. Some of us flow with the cycles of the Moon, others resist them. If we go with the flow of the lunar cycle rather than struggling against it, and also take the time to try to understand our own Moon sign qualities, we will begin to discover harmony in our lives and feel at one with nature, too.

Lunar Cycles in the Horoscope

As we've seen, it takes about four weeks, or twenty-eight days, for the Moon to move around the zodiac, spending about two days in each sign. Remember the main phases: Dark of the New Moon, Waxing Moon, Full Moon and Waning Moon (see page 34). There are other cycles too, such as the cycles of the Moon as she moves through the astrological year, marked by pivotal times such as the Full or New Moon in each sign, and by solar and lunar eclipses. But for you, the most significant thing about the Moon in astrology is where she was in your horoscope when you were born, and what phase of the Moon you were born under.

How to Discover Your Moon Sign

Most of us know which 'Sun sign' (also known as our 'star sign') we are, as it's very easy to find out by looking at your horoscope online, or in a magazine where the accompanying dates are listed. (Of course, if you were born 'on the cusp' – a day when the Sun moved into or out of a sign – then you may have to ask a professional to check by drawing up a complete birth chart.)

Finding out your Moon sign can be a little trickier. Unless you are really into astrology, working out the Moon's position at the time of your birth is best left to a computer or an easy-to-understand internet site, where you can enter your birth details and get the answer. (There is a list of easy-to-access sites who will calculate your Moon sign for free on page 289).

Once you know in which sign the Moon was located when you were born, you can read the following information to help you understand not only more about yourself, but also how to use that information to enhance and empower you. On page 187 you will discover how to work with the various cycles of the Moon in tandem with your own lunar placement.

Your Moon Sign and its Lunar Phase

As well as knowing your Moon sign, it is also important to discover under which phase of the Moon you were born. This is because the lunar phase, whether Full, Waxing, Waning or New, describes the way you react to life and other people on a daily basis. For example, you may be born with the Moon in Capricorn, but if you were born during a Full Moon phase (which exaggerates feelings), you will probably be more emotional than you'd like to be around a Full Moon, even though your Moon in Capricorn thrives in a calm, controlled environment.

If you were born during the Full Moon:
Generally, you're very open and have an emotionally receptive attitude. You soak up ideas and other people's feelings. During a Full Moon, you usually feel more vulnerable and more emotional, and may overreact to situations.

If you were born during a Waning Moon phase:
You are able to analyse and reflect carefully before committing yourself and have great stamina and inner emotional strength. With others, you're a little cautious about revealing too much about yourself, and find it hard to be really honest about your needs.

If you were born during the Dark of the New Moon phase:

You may be psychic, but you're a bit of a loner and prefer small groups of people to grand social events. You're good at keeping secrets, and you don't say much about your needs. However, you do feel things deeply and are highly intuitive.

If you were born during a Waxing Moon phase:

Creative and inspiring, you're always ready to take a leap in the dark or set off on a new adventure, complete tasks and finalise decisions. You need life to be fun, carefree and undemanding.

Working Out Your Moon Phase

To be sure about the phase of the Moon you were born under, please refer to an astrological website, which will give you information about your horoscope (see page 289 for a list of recommended websites), or try using the calculation below.

Work Out Your Moon Phase with a Little Simple Maths

First, you need to look at an image of your birth chart and check what degree your Sun is in its sign. This is usually readily apparent when you look at your birth chart on the internet: the degree is usually listed beside the symbol for the Sun.

When you look at your birth chart, please note that the signs of the zodiac revolve anticlockwise. So, starting from the Sun's placement, always calculate the Moon's phase working in an anticlockwise direction.

Let's take an example. Say you have the Sun at 20 degrees Taurus.

Is it a Dark of the New Moon phase?

If your Moon is within 5 degrees of either side of the Sun (so between 15 and 25 degrees Taurus), you were born during the Dark of the New Moon phase.

Is it a Full Moon phase?

The culmination of the Full Moon falls exactly opposite the Sun, but again within a range of 5 degrees either way. So, in our example with the Sun at 20 degrees Taurus, the Full Moon would be exactly opposite, at 20 degrees Scorpio.

If you look at a horoscope, you will see that exactly opposite the sun in Taurus is the sign of Scorpio. If you were to draw a line exactly 180 degrees across the circle from the Sun, you'll get to 20 degrees Scorpio.

Counting from the Taurus Sun, and working anticlockwise, if your Moon falls within 5 degrees on either side of the Full Moon degree (in this case, between 15 and 25 degrees Scorpio), you are a Full Moon phase person.

Is it a Waxing Moon phase?

If, working anticlockwise, your natal Moon falls 5 degrees or more after your Sun and 5 degrees before the Full Moon, you were born in a Waxing Moon phase.

In our example, if the natal Moon falls somewhere between the range of 25 degrees Taurus and 15 degrees Scorpio, let's say at 8 degrees Libra, you are a Waxing Moon phase person.

Is it a Waning Moon phase?

If, working anticlockwise, your natal Moon falls 5 degrees or more after the Full Moon, and 5 degrees before your Sun, then you were born in a Waning Moon phase.

In our example, if the natal Moon falls somewhere between the range of 25 degrees Scorpio and 15 degrees Taurus, let's say at 10 degrees Aquarius, you are a Waning Moon phase person.

Ritual Empowerments for Your Lunar Phase

To empower you with the positive characteristics of your natal lunar phase, and to diminish any negative traits, here are specific rituals to perform depending on which lunar phase you were born in.

If You Were Born During the Dark of the New Moon

Whatever sign of the zodiac your Moon is in, being born in this phase heightens your intuitive powers and sensitivity to outer influences or experiences.

CANDLE RITUAL FOR EMPOWERING POSITIVE QUALITIES

As the Moon turns to her dark phase, many of us feel the need to reflect or look inward, to regroup or reaffirm what we might need to activate in the next lunar cycle. Yet, as you were born at this time, you know instinctively how to prepare yourself, whether to withdraw and reflect, or to set the wheels in motion for the next lunar cycle, or to get ready for the next 'wake-up call'.

The positive side of this Dark of the New Moon phase is that you become highly intuitive and can get deeply in touch with your spiritual self as the deeper, unconscious part of you becomes more accessible. Through dreams, flashes of insight or enlightened moments, you will come to know the truth of the matter. Make use of this time to strengthen your intuitive or psychic powers through meditation, or by performing this positive Dark of the New Moon candle ritual.

You will need:

> 3 white candles
> a large mirror

1. On the evening of the Dark of the New Moon, take the candles and place them in a row in front of the mirror.
2. Light the candles and gaze into the reflected glow. As you do so, meditate for a few minutes, repeating in your mind what truly matters to you right now, and what your intentions are for the next lunar cycle.
3. When you are ready, blow out the candles. You will be focused and prepared for the next stage of your lunar journey.

ROSEBUD SPELL FOR DIMINISHING NEGATIVE TRAITS

The phase that feels most uncomfortable for you is the end of a Waxing phase, towards the culmination of a Full Moon. This is because all emotions, feelings and reactions are on a high for many people, and in nature, there's an energetic sense of getting things finalised, a need to get organised and do practical things, which can unsettle your more introverted, feeling-focused world. To diminish or reduce a tendency to overreact or overthink, perform the following ritual just before the Full Moon.

You will need:

a bowl of water
a handful of rosebuds

1. Place the bowl of water on a window ledge or outside if possible. The important thing is that it's in a place exposed to the moonlight (even if it's cloudy!).

2. Gaze into the water. As you do so, sprinkle the rosebuds into the bowl and say: 'With this love, I give out to my lunar pathway my faith that all will be good for me this Full Moon.' Leave overnight and your sense of calm will be restored during this phase.

If You Were Born During a Waxing Moon

Whatever sign of the zodiac your Moon was in, the Waxing Moon phase enhances your creative skills, and your ability to think on your feet and activate new projects.

CRYSTAL RITUAL FOR EMPOWERING POSITIVE QUALITIES

For most people, the Waxing crescent Moon, lazing in the sky in her gentle arc, suggests new things to come: perhaps a change of attitude to something more positive and fruitful. If you were born under a Waxing Moon, you instinctively react to this phase by becoming more creative and energised, ready to set out and explore new horizons, whether of the mind, body or spirit.

During this phase, you can start new projects and know that they will bring you success, as long as the majority of the work is finished before the culmination of the Full

Moon. It's important during this phase to give out information, to make contacts with those who can inspire or help you succeed, or to instigate new romance, if that's what you're looking for. Follow the Waxing Moon ritual below to maximise all your creative powers.

You will need:

a piece of white quartz
your journal or a piece of paper

1. On an evening during a Waxing Moon phase, take up your journal or piece of paper and write down one wish. Make it clear exactly what you are looking for, whether that is more creativity, good contacts or romance.
2. When you have written your wish, close your journal or fold the paper into four, then place the white quartz on top of it. As you do so, repeat four times (to channel the energy of the four elements): 'This book, this wish, this look, this Moon; all will be mine to have soon.'
3. Thank the Moon for her help and leave the message and crystal in place until after the Full Moon.

SEED-SOWING RITUAL FOR
DIMINISHING NEGATIVE TRAITS

Is there a downside to this highly creative energy, you wonder? Yes, there certainly is: those born at this time are often overly optimistic, believing they can get away with anything. The retreating energy of the Waning Moon phase can diminish your creative hopes, and you may find your expectations haven't been met. Use this time to think about the creative seeds you've sown, or to take pride in what you have achieved, rather than judge yourself. Perform the following ritual during a Waning phase to revive your spirit of adventure.

You will need:

a red candle
a handful of poppy or sunflower seeds
a pot of earth (such as a flowerpot or a plastic
    container)
a stick or wand

1. On a Waning Moon evening, light the candle on your sacred table or altar and place your ingredients in front of it.
2. Sprinkle some of the seeds onto the earth, saying the following as you do so:

    'The time is right to sow my seeds,
    For wisdom, truth and newest deeds,

Which will be done in two weeks' time;
This is my chance to really shine.'

3. Move some of the earth over the seeds or push
    the seeds gently down beneath the surface. You
    are not expecting them to grow: this is a sym-
    bolic gesture.
4. Gaze into the candle flame for a few minutes to
    meditate on the 'mental and creative' seeds you
    have also sown, then blow out the candle. This
    ritual will revive your creativity or energy for a
    new start.

If You Were Born During a Full Moon

Whatever sign of the zodiac your Moon is in, people born
under a Full Moon are said to be highly emotional. All
theatre and drama, they have exaggerated moods and
thoughts which they tend to unleash on those around
them; yet, because of all that, they live life to the full.

MALACHITE AND MOONSTONE SPELL FOR EMPOWERING POSITIVE QUALITIES

Whatever sign you were born under, if you were born
under a Full Moon you will feel very deeply and strongly
about life and love, and also be very open to other people's
moods and feelings. As the Full Moon approaches you may
feel burdened by other people's psychic energy and, as it cul-
minates, you may feel a strong sense of relief that you don't

have to carry the weight of 'feeling' for at least another few weeks. The benefit of possessing such depth of emotion is that, if you learn to love this part of yourself, you will come to know that the world isn't just about logical analysis, but more about trusting your deepest gut instincts. You will also have a natural ability to complete projects or achieve goals.

Embrace all the moods you have, whether good or bad. Look at them as a bundle of energy that interweaves, like yin and yang, and place no judgement upon that energy. The joy of having heightened emotions is that you instinctively understand the qualities of other people's lunar needs, too. To enhance your innate ability to finalise deals or confirm a positive outcome in love and romance, perform the following ritual just before the Full Moon.

You will need:

> a white candle
> a green candle
> a piece of malachite
> a piece of moonstone
> 3 basil leaves

1. On the evening of the Full Moon, place the candles on a window ledge or another place that is exposed to the moonlight (it doesn't matter if it's cloudy). Place the malachite in front of the white candle, and the moonstone in front of the green candle.
2. Light the candles, and finally place a leaf of basil beside each crystal, and the third leaf in between.

3. Focus on a specific issue you would like resolved and repeat it in your mind or out loud while you hold first the moonstone then the malachite.

4. Finally take the basil leaves and pass them quickly through each candle flame to release your intention to the Moon.

LIGHT RITUAL FOR DIMINISHING NEGATIVE TRAITS

As a Full Moon child you are highly emotional, but the Dark of the New Moon phase can diminish your instinctive belief in your mission. This is a 'black' time, when your feelings turn inwards and you may feel particularly vulnerable, less confident and unsure of yourself. To augment self-understanding and to help you get through this phase, follow this ritual to balance the heightened emotions of the Full Moon and help you stay focused and serene.

You will need:

a sage smudging stick

1. On the evening of the Dark of the New Moon, light the smudging stick. Take the stick and walk around every corner and room of your home, waving the stick gently around to cleanse all energy.

2. As you do so, repeat this chant: 'I believe in myself and my energy is rekindled throughout this space and for the next lunar cycle.'

If You Were Born During a Waning Moon

Whatever sign of the zodiac your Moon is in, Waning Moon people have what I would call a 'stoical' approach to life and love. Philosophical and accepting, you are aware that life and love need to be worked at.

RED FIRE SPELL FOR EMPOWERING POSITIVE QUALITIES

Your ability to see life from many different perspectives means you get things done, but you also have the instinctive patience and inner resolve to wait for the appropriate changing energy before you instigate a plan or new project. With the Waning Moon, you naturally reflect on, revive or reinvent ideas, or re-establish the power of your own intuition. You are adept at meditation, self-analysis and controlling your thoughts to come to a conclusion about your future. To empower your innate talent for universal understanding, perform the following ritual during the Waning Moon.

You will need:

3 red candles
a large mirror

3 × 60-cm (2-foot) lengths of red ribbon
a heavy book

1. On an evening during the Waning Moon, light the
    red candles in front of the mirror at your altar or
    sacred table.
2. Take up the three ribbons and knot them together
    at one end. Place this end under the book to hold
    it down. Plait the ribbons, and as you do so repeat
    this chant:

    'With ribbons red I start my thread,
    To bring me joy and purpose bold,
    Enhance my powers of psychic gold
    And make success of all that's said.'

3. When you have finished plaiting and chanting,
    blow out the candles to petition your request
    to the Moon.

TRUE VISION SPELL FOR
DIMINISHING NEGATIVE TRAITS

The downside of being born under a Waning Moon is a
tendency to overthink, or feel you're not good enough
when those bright, creative Waxing Moon achievers
always seem to have luck on their side. During a Waxing
Moon, those charming self-starters are often in the limelight. Rather than worrying about what others think of

you, or focusing on what others are 'gaining', try to see that your wisdom and knowledge is worth just as much, as is your ability to maintain a cool discipline. Perform the ritual below during a Waxing Moon to revitalise your self-value and self-esteem.

You will need:

a moonstone
a gold (or gold-coloured) ring

1. On the evening of the Waxing Moon, take the moonstone and place it on a window ledge or a place exposed to the moonlight (even if cloudy).
2. Close your eyes. Hold the gold ring in your writing hand and touch the moonstone with the other hand. As you do so, say the following spell:

   'I am truth and light, my vision clear,
   My values firm, my future dear,
   All that I am, I love to be,
   So others will see such power in me.'

3. Open your eyes and place the ring beside the moonstone. Leave them in place until the Full Moon to empower you with self-worth and creative spirit.

Chapter 8

Your Moon Sign

In your astrological birth chart, the Moon is of equal importance to the Sun when it comes to defining your personality (see page 179). The position of the Moon, and its relation to other planets, also reveals details about our relationships, feelings and needs. As the Moon moves so quickly around the complete zodiac (taking about two and a half days to move through one sign), its transits can also influence or mirror events and experiences in your life on a daily basis.

This chapter is devoted to discovering your personality and character traits depending on your Moon's natal birth sign, and how to work with this energy to make the best of yourself. Each section also includes a tip to promote positive energy, and advice on which crystal to wear or carry to enhance well-being.

You will find out more about:

> Your emotions, feelings, moods, sensitivity
> and intuition

What you need to be your best self
How you react to life and love
Your comfort zones (in social or work settings)
and your attitude to body
What you need to feel a sense of belonging,
family and home
What you need in love relationships
The Moon's lesson for you

Moon in Aries

Moods/Feelings
Your moods are fiery and extreme.

Sensitivity
You are acutely aware of changing energy.

Intuition
Your intuition is strongly felt, but often ignored.

Moon Crystal: Red Carnelian
Wear it as jewellery (or carry it in a pouch) during a
Waxing Moon phase, or when you have to impress some-
one with your dynamic spirit of adventure.

Needs
If you can maintain a lifestyle filled with action and adventure that gives free rein to your independent spirit, you'll
be fulfilling your lunar need for space and freedom. Some

may say you are self-centred, and everything you do is tinged with an impatient attitude, but as long as you're given the space to do your own thing, you'll be loyal and true. You need to make your own choices and decisions, even if they sometimes lead you down a difficult path. A bit of a warrior, you'll fight on behalf of other people's need for security, as long as it doesn't interfere with your own. You need a dynamic love relationship where you can express your desires whenever you feel like it. Whether others will agree is another matter.

Reactions

You react to things people say or do at high speed, which means you can be impulsive and make hasty judgements, often regretting your actions or words later. If you have the space to come and go as you please, you'll feel more secure in a relationship and become less reactionary. Acting without thinking or reflecting can often lead you into situations that create tension and turmoil, yet, in an unconscious way, it may be that you also need that kind of drama in your vivacious life.

Comfort Zones

Although you love getting out and about and attending social gatherings, you're restless and can't sit still for long. You have an innate talent for leading the pack, and if you are chosen by those around you at work to lead new projects, you shine and take control of any situation. If you're held up at work, though, or delayed on a train or plane, you are likely to vent your anger on someone or something, and find it hard to keep your thoughts to yourself. The best working life for you is one with lots of personal space and no routine or demands.

Belonging, Family and Home

You belong to yourself. Although you can easily bond to one other person, you're not particularly a home-loving animal, preferring to maintain a sense of independence rather than belong to any clan, club or group. Family is important, as long as you have the freedom to come and go, doing your own thing when you choose, with no commitments. This can be seen as selfish, but it's more that, with this intense sense of self, there also comes an understanding of how to promote other people's individuality. You would probably do well to have someone else to clean up after you, as the last thing you have time for is chores.

The Moon's Lesson

Don't give up on your individuality for the sake of others, but do be aware of, and compassionate about, their needs.

Tip to Boost Positive Lunar Energy

Keep a piece of tiger's eye on your work desk, or in the drawer, to maximise your organisational and leadership skills.

Moon in Taurus

Moods/Feelings
Your feelings appear controlled on the surface, but rumble beneath.

Sensitivity
You feel things deeply, despite your hard-nosed attitude.

Intuition
You trust your gut instinct.

Moon Crystal: Pink Tourmaline
Carry the crystal in your pocket on a romantic date and you'll get the results you hope for.

Needs
With an acute awareness of the reality of life's material problems, you need security and a reliable income. You also need an exclusive relationship with closeness, sensual togetherness, consistency and reliable loving. Once you have that kind of comfort, you would move the Earth for someone if you had to. Resistant to change, your drive for constant attention and routine can overwhelm others, and then your possessive streak takes over. Staying in control of your emotions and your money go hand in hand, so if you feel financially fragile or vulnerable, your mood will follow suit. This often results in vengeful words, or feeling you are being betrayed.

Reactions

Although you instinctively 'know' how other people are feeling or thinking, you take your time before reacting or responding to them, preferring to make them feel enchanted and welcome before you let them get too close. This means you react to romantic situations in a very laid-back, seductive way. If you're let down or feel misled, resentment builds up slowly but surely, and you can explode with accusations or blame, often accusing the other person of your own controlling tactics.

Comfort Zones

You are best suited to working in a creative environment where you neither have to take the lead, nor end up being merely a team player. That means you often find yourself working freelance or being self-employed, as long as you are able to interact with others and show off your skills. Flaunting your talents makes you feel good about yourself, but it is even better if you receive unprecedented praise. In social situations you shine in the kitchen, and if your culinary skills are admired by friends, colleagues and family, you're in seventh heaven. Out and about, you prefer to remain fairly discreet, and would rather take the back seat in the taxi than chat to the driver.

Belonging, Family and Home

Family life is hugely important to you, and if you're in charge of the home set-up and finances, including everyone's piggy banks, you'll make sure everyone is happy too. You want to belong to a clan or group, even if you're single, and joining a holiday art class or other creative vacation will put you in touch with the kind of people who make you feel at home. Your belongings are treasures, and you're known to hoard everything under the Sun, often finding it hard to declutter or move home.

The Moon's Lesson

Try not to control everyone; continue being your generous, loving self without making demands.

Tip to Boost Positive Lunar Energy

You can be so preoccupied with how to impress others or look good, you forget about the big wide world out there. So, wear an aventurine bracelet or talisman to help you see life from a wider perspective.

Moon in Gemini

Moods/Feelings

Your moods are scattered, unpredictable and changeable.

Sensitivity

You may appear oblivious to others, but you're easily hurt.

Intuition

You often muddle intuition with your vivid imagination.

Moon Crystal: Yellow Citrine

Place a piece of citrine in your desk drawer during a new crescent Moon to promote fascinating contacts and fun.

Needs

For someone who tends to avoid your feelings, you can become quite moody if things are not as jolly and cheerful as you would like. You need admiring attention, you need to feel attractive, you need to have fun, and you thrive on constant change. Light-hearted and often whimsical, you know, deep down, there is a dark twin within you, but you rarely allow yourself to get stuck in that emotionally dark place for long. A cool, laid-back partner is just the tonic you need.

Reactions

Your quick response in all forms of communication can spark off temperamental partners and confused colleagues. Sometimes you open your mouth or send a text message before you think things through, not considering the consequences. Later, you respond to your own reactions either with regret, trying to patch things up, or by shrugging your shoulders and moving on, in the hope it will all be forgotten. You don't bear grudges, but many bear them towards you due to your rather flippant attitude. Romantic advances or seductive admirers tempt you to give too much away about yourself, and make you feel used.

Comfort Zones

You are at your best in social or work situations where you have a neutral status. Being the boss or standing out from the crowd is not really your thing, and you make a good team player who can multi-task and get jobs done before anyone else has had time to change their mind. You're most comfortable when out and about and not stuck in one place for too long. Lengthy dinner parties spent sitting around the table are not for you; you prefer the more dynamic interplay of a group of people in a bar or pub, or a ride in the forest, or being down by the sea. Anything goes, and that's mostly to keep your highly active mind constantly in motion.

Belonging, Family and Home

You don't really like to belong to anyone, or anything. A bit of a nomad, you're more likely to enjoy a free-ranging independent existence with few ties. So, although your family are much-loved and important to your deeper self, they are also usually a burden, and you prefer a sense of non-attachment, with no commitments made for anniversaries, weddings or family get-togethers. However, you are great fun to have around if everyone else can accept your mercurial nature. Your home is usually a bit of a mess: you're not fond of the drudgery of life, or the cleaning rota. You will muck in and then muck out as quickly as you possibly can, as there are always more interesting things to do.

The Moon's Lesson
Learn to focus your busy mind on one thing and you will achieve great results.

Tip to Boost Positive Lunar Energy
Revitalise the lost arts of communication. Perfect calligraphy, champion the restoration of longhand, indulge in music, poetry or love letters. Use the natural touch of personal script and evocative words to get you in touch with your inspirational thoughts.

Moon in Cancer

Moods/Feelings
You have emotional moods that fluctuate with the Moon cycle.

Sensitivity
Your sensitivity is acute. You are vulnerable and empathetic.

Intuition
You are deeply knowing, psychic, aware.

Moon Crystal: Selenite
Hold a piece of selenite in front of the flame of a white candle and focus on your desires to maximise happiness.

Needs

Anyone with the Moon in Cancer is going to feel particularly susceptible to the day-to-day changes of the lunar cycles, and this is often the hardest placement for the astrological Moon. However, the good news is that, because you are so aware of the moods, feelings and emotions of others, you can work with this energy and avoid getting too needy by helping others with their own issues. You tend to be naturally sympathetic and can put yourself in other people's shoes. Instead of depending on other people, you need to show them that feelings and sensitivity are natural and can be embraced.

Reactions

When someone whirls past you in a good or bad mood, you sense it in the air, and you may react with concern or carelessness, depending on your own mood. You know when someone is hurt, unhappy, proud or carefree, because you are all these things too, or have been them at one time or another. So usually you react in the most appropriate way, giving the right signals back and not getting defensive. However, there are times it is all too much for you and, during the Waning Moon, you want to run and hide in your shell and not be distracted by the energies around you.

Comfort Zones

You love to nurture others, and feel most comfortable giving presents and being 'mum' at the dinner party, family outing or work place. Although some may say you have an ulterior motive, compensating perhaps for a lack of self-esteem, you know that if you're in familiar surroundings, you will always give your best. At work, you can be both team player and boss, as long as you feel you are part of the 'gang' or at least have the opportunity to mother some part of the team or take newcomers under your wing. You also love spending hours helping out in other people's kitchens, gossiping and giving advice.

Belonging, Family and Home
You long to belong to something or someone, and also have other people belong to you in the same sort of 'clannish', homely way. A consistent home life is essential to you. Depending on the other planets in your chart, that can be the grandest or humblest home in the country, but hearth, warmth, comfort and natural surroundings are a must. Family is also a must, but the little word 'mother' can be a big issue. You may have a mother or a mother figure in your family who means a lot to you, whether good or bad. If the latter, you often resist their influence, and have to learn to mother yourself.

The Moon's Lesson
You need to learn to voice your feelings at the right moment: don't hold back, or you will only resent others.

Tip to Boost Positive Lunar Energy
Being psychic means that you pick up outside stress, whether from others or the local environment. Protect yourself by wearing your Moon sign crystal or talisman.

Each Full Moon, hold a piece of selenite to connect to the lunar power and stop you feeling vulnerable around others.

Moon in Leo

Moods/Feelings
Your moods are dramatic, bold, full on, theatrical.

Sensitivity
You are reactionary and fearless.

Intuition
Your sense of intuition is confused and you are highly imaginative.

Moon Crystal: Tiger's Eye
Place the crystal near your front door so that every time you pass by, positive energy permeates your home.

Needs
As long as you have faithful friends, family and a partner, you'll show off their talents and qualities as if they were your own. In love, you need someone who showers you with affection, strokes your brow when you're sprawled out like a hot lion after a busy day at the office, and makes you feel good to be you. Purring with pride, you can exaggerate your feelings and strut around like a caged cat, so you need to express those theatrical moods through art, music or being the star of some show. Try not to stamp

your feet if your needs aren't met. If you have the space and understanding from others to allow you to go off and be centre stage, your neediness blows over very quickly.

Reactions

If people are nervy, sad, distressed or in a sulk, you immediately feel the bad energy and usually attempt to switch their mood to a more joyful one. You react badly to moody people because their negativity has a draining effect on your *joie de vivre*. You want life to be a joyous affair, and so you may overreact and blow off steam to clear the air. In a lively, social environment, you're the first to take centre stage. As long as people are praising you or admiring your strengths, you react with genuine compassion and willingness to please others.

Comfort Zones

Lions are family orientated, but they also hunt alone. This is very reflective of your innate need for a huge family and social life, yet also your need, at times, for solitude and peace. In social situations you shine, outclass others with your talents and appear larger than life. Although this is where you feel most comfortable, it is also where you might discover that you are not the only Moon in Leo in the room. Any sense of rivalry, and you'll move to another spotlight. The same goes for work: as long as you are running the show, or are the favourite for doing what you do, you will feel your best.

Belonging, Family and Home

Being larger than life, you enjoy having an entourage of family and friends around you, but there are times when you like to roam alone. Not for any dark motive, but just to get a sense of that deeper sense of belonging to oneself that is at the heart of every true lion's nature. You are loyal and passionate about the world and everything in it. Your home may be all bling on the surface, with your home decor displaying your taste for luxurious living; but inside you, the richest chambers of self-acceptance are to be found.

The Moon's Lesson

You need to learn that there are other people who shine just as much as you do, and accept that, although you are special, you are not the only one on stage.

Tip to Boost Positive Lunar Energy

Although you're well aware you're already a bit of a star, take up yoga, invest in a personal trainer and treat yourself to a complete makeover to maximise your appearance and put you in the limelight.

Moon in Virgo

Moods/Feelings

You are cool yet scattered, poised yet vulnerable.

Sensitivity
You are highly strung, but compassionate.

Intuition
Sometimes your intuition is spot on, but sometimes you are lost.

Moon Crystal: Blue Lace Agate
To ensure success in your career or profession, wear this crystal during important rendezvous and when meeting new contacts.

Needs
You tend to keep your true feelings hidden. Your emotions make you nervous, and so does unpredictable behaviour in others. OK, so you don't make a fuss about your needs, but they still need sorting out, sifting and cultivating. The problem with emotion is it's alien to your lunar need for the pure, simple and tempered nature of your lunar landscape. In romantic relationships, you need someone with an equally cool approach, perhaps even an intellectual one, where you have time to work out what love and life means to you, rather than being overworked by it. In other words, you need a partner or love relationship where the barometer is set to an even temperature, with an undisturbed routine, and where spontaneity and the unpredictable are replaced by civilised living and rational behaviour.

Reactions

You react to life and love in a cool and aloof manner. You don't like drama and you keep your wits about you, preferring an objective analysis of the situation to a flaming row. If your new lover doesn't phone or text, rather than overreact, you work out all the possible reasons for why they haven't called, and this in itself becomes a fascinating exercise in logistics. The first time you meet a potential partner, you notice every flaw and detail about them, usually as a defensive reaction so that later you have ammunition with which to criticise them if facing rejection. With a calm, orderly, processed attempt to avoid conflict and dark emotions, most people find you comfortingly honest, and a calm influence.

Comfort Zones

Feeling most at home in a stress-free working environment, you prefer working hard behind the scenes. Although you work well in a team, you are most comfortable with a high level of responsibility, so you are best left to edit other people's ideas or projects rather than sell them. In social situations, you feel relaxed as the discreet host, or the guest who helps with the washing up. In a gathering of friends, you may appear cool, and not exactly the life and soul of the party, but whatever you say is said with integrity, and is usually highly valued. In a relationship, you are happiest making love between crisp white sheets, or indulging in a romantic dinner with candles and champagne.

Belonging, Family and Home

Traditional values matter most to you in all aspects of your life and, as long as you are in control of domestic arrangements, you create a harmonious family life. In fact, your home must be orderly, crisp, clean and uncluttered, and you may even be a bit of a Feng Shui addict. As soon as there's any sign of chaos or mess, you're on the warpath – or you just quietly clear it up yourself. Family members must understand the rules of the household, and your mildly obsessive desire for wholesome living.

The Moon's Lesson

You need to learn that there is order in chaos, and that between black and white there are shades of grey.

Tip to Boost Positive Lunar Energy

You say you're sceptical of anything supernatural, but you do have a secret longing to manifest your own intentions, or you wouldn't be reading this book. Carry a piece of citrine with you to enhance all communication, success and progress, and to honour your deepest desires.

Moon in Libra

Moods/Feelings

You are cool, rational and serene.

Sensitivity

You have high aesthetic awareness.

Intuition

Your intuition is strong, but often ignored.

Moon Crystal: Blue Sapphire

Place a piece of blue sapphire under your pillow during a
Full Moon to bring you the love you deserve.

Needs

You have a natural gift for making other people feel
relaxed in your company, but you avoid confrontation or
emotional turmoil at all costs. When your own feelings
arise, you try to analyse them away. You need a love relationship that is complete, and where you feel totally part of
a couple, rather than one of two autonomous individuals.
This desire to merge means that you are always willing to
please and ready to compromise just to keep others happy,
sometimes at the expense of yourself. Your need for a
beautiful partner, or charming and elegant surroundings,
set the bar high, and others find it difficult to live up to
your idealistic needs. But with a little humility, you can
find the near-perfect world you seek.

Reactions

You react to romantic circumstances with genuine warmth
and a charming smile, instinctively knowing how to please
someone to get the kind of energy and flow that maintains
harmony. You are quite seductive and know deep down
that this kind of reaction means you can later get your
way. Your ability to compromise comes naturally to you,
but it can be your own worst enemy. Any negativity from

others causes you to instinctively retreat rather than speak up. You may be a champion for justice and an ambassador for others, but when it comes to your own inner harmony being threatened you'd rather run a mile. Later you may resent others, blaming them for your passivity.

Comfort Zones

To enhance your sense of joy and a feeling of well-being, surround yourself with beautiful interiors: a home in which you can showcase your talents, and a workplace which is aesthetically pleasing. If you don't live or work in a harmonious environment, you will have to create one around you. The same goes for your friends and social life. Your lover or partner must be a perfect match or considered pretty, youthful and beautiful; they must conform to your ideals and grace your presence with their charm. At your most relaxed, you thrive in a workplace where everyone works as equals and there is no competition.

Belonging, Family and Home

Although you're happy in groups, you prefer a merger of two minds and a genuine committed partnership; after all, two's company, and three can be a bit of a crowd. Home is, of course, where you're in your element. This is the place to showcase your eye for beauty and your sense of style, and a space where you innately know how to create a perfect balance. You love your family, but if they don't respect your need for harmony, you may find you don't have as much control over them as you do your interior decoration.

The Moon's Lesson

You need to understand that you are not joined at the hip to your partner, but that you are two separate individuals.

Tip to Boost Positive Lunar Energy

Secretly you yearn for some kind of 'spiritual' connection. You don't have to believe; just learn and discover that the very mysteries you fear are actually within you. Hold two moonstones every Full Moon to reconnect to lunar love and power.

Moon in Scorpio

Moods/Feelings

Your moods are intense, passionate and extreme.

Sensitivity

You have a profound sensitivity to others' feelings

Intuition

Your intuition is powerful and always spot on.

Moon Crystal: Obsidian

Carry a piece of obsidian in a pouch during a Waning Moon to promote your talents and seed opportunity for the next lunar cycle.

Needs

In love relationships you need a partner who understands how deeply and strongly you feel. You feel both intense love and intense hate, and they are not mutually exclusive. You need to get to know someone thoroughly before you give much away about yourself. Once you decide someone is trustworthy and right for you, you have to be needed more than you need them. Fiercely individual, you are often jealous and possessive, but you don't show these darker emotions unless pushed by mistrust or betrayal, when you either resort to double standards yourself, or use that well-known sting in your tail. You need a lot of alone time to process your emotions and to rise from any ashes like a phoenix. Although you are a loner, you still need a few very special people in your life who are loyal, reliable and true.

Reactions

You instantly understand other people's deepest needs and know instinctively who they are. You don't give away much about yourself, and yet you continue to probe others for their motives and secrets. In love relationships, if you argue with your partner you can sit and brood for days, processing your emotions until you're ready to come out of your dark place, usually with renewed passion and love. However, negativity from work colleagues or in your social network can bring out the worst in you, and in these areas you react by turning the tables on others, or ruthlessly manipulating them.

Comfort Zones

Quite frankly, you feel out of your comfort zone most of the time, because the Moon in Scorpio psyche is not suited to social occasions, working environments and the general pace of modern life. What suits you best are the places where most people don't go, such as the lonely tops of mountains, silent canyons, the wide open sea, an empty beach or a dark wood or forest. Nature and all its power enhances your sense of well-being, and helps you get in touch with your deepest sense of self and your connection to the universe.

Belonging, Family and Home

You enjoy solitary work and play, and your home is private, secluded and intimate. You're not a great one for a big family and prefer a few close pals rather than a wild social life. If you're tempted to join a group, it's most likely to be something taboo, prohibited or cultish. You're renowned for getting involved in clandestine affairs, yet your family role will appear traditional and above reproach on the surface. Such covert secrets are powerful and give you a sense of belonging only to yourself, and not to anyone or anything else.

The Moon's Lesson

You need to learn to trust others rather than being constantly suspicious of their motives; that way you will learn to trust yourself better too.

Tip to Boost Positive Lunar Energy

The Moon in Scorpio thrives on solitude or solitary pursuits, so try and go for long walks alone, work out in the gym, write a novel or paint a masterpiece. Carry obsidian with you to enhance your self-reliant nature.

Moon in Sagittarius

Moods/Feelings

Your moods are fiery, haphazard, dynamic.

Sensitivity

You are unconcerned, aloof, undiscerning.

Intuition

Your intuition is erratic: sometimes spot on, sometimes off by a mile.

Moon Crystal: Lapis Lazuli

On your travels, keep a stone in your bag or wear one as jewellery to attract good intentions wherever you go.

Needs

The word 'need' doesn't exactly sit well in your vocabulary. In fact, it's what you don't need to feel comfortable and secure that really matters. For example, you don't need commitments, you don't need to feel responsible for your actions – and you don't need to *feel* too much at all. You do, however, need adventure, excitement, passion and spontaneity. You need wild, unconditional love. Although you make promises on impulse, you rarely keep them, finding that something you promised two hours ago doesn't sound like such a great idea a few hours later. Your biggest need is to be true to your dynamic self, and have an inspirational partner or friend too.

Reactions

You usually react suddenly and often without consideration for other people's feelings. Feelings are human, after all, and you would rather run with the wolves or the gods than be just another human being. Living on an idealistic plane, being dragged down to the muddy waters of reality pulls down your spirit too. But if there's negative energy in the room, you attempt to turn it into positive energy, and if there's a positive charge around you, you'll become your best self: extrovert, fun-loving and totally carefree.

Comfort Zones

Your comfort zones include the great outdoors, challenges, exploration and travelling the world, or at least keeping in constant motion. Of course, if you have an earthy Sun sign (star sign), like Taurus, you might feel torn between a desire to flop on the sofa and the urge to get out in the pouring rain and dig the garden. If anyone knocks your spirit of adventure, or sticks you behind a desk, that kind of trap will push your rebellious buttons to get you out of the door faster than you walked in.

Belonging, Family and Home

Belonging to no one except yourself, it's hard for you to enjoy a sense of traditional 'family' life. However, you may be suited to a very unusual family, perhaps spread across several continents, requiring long-distance travel, and where all is spontaneous and last-minute. Your home, if you manage to live in a fixed one, rather than a mobile home or caravan, will be filled with useful things, but not much else. You don't need accessories or possessions. When you travel, you travel light, keeping yourself commitment-free.

The Moon's Lesson

You need to learn that not everyone is as enthusiastic about your ideas as you are. Come down to earth a little and see that no one, not even you, can live up to your ideals.

Tip to Boost Positive Lunar Energy

Expand your amazing mind with Eastern philosophy, world mythology or history. Armed with that kind of knowledge, you'll always have something to talk about and can revel in being the centre of attention wherever you go on your travels. During a Waxing Moon, place a piece of turquoise under your bed to bring you successful dreams.

Moon in Capricorn

Moods/Feelings

You are composed, poised and level-headed.

Sensitivity
Your sensitivity is acute, but often ignored.

Intuition
Your intuition is strong, trusted and well-grounded.

Moon Crystal: Onyx
Place a piece of onyx above the main entrance to your office or workspace to enhance all business dealings.

Needs
The power of this lunar placement gives you stamina, resilience and an independent spirit. You may not like your darker emotions, but you learn to work with them and acknowledge them for what they are. But are you actually needier than most people think? Probably, as you don't give much away. You're not like a fiery type who explodes and tells the world how they're feeling: you're the one who stays cool in a crisis. It may seem like a contradiction, but you also need a lot of attention and praise to feel worthy. You need to be cared for and yet given the freedom to make your own way in the world. You are one of the most reliable and trustworthy Moon signs around.

Reactions
Rarely do you overreact to other people's emotional outbursts or tempers. You are quick to sense both negative and positive energy in any environment, but smart enough to know how to protect yourself from anyone or anything which could upset your mood. You trust your intuition

and know that it can work in your favour, particularly when it comes to your career, love life, social climbing and personal success.

Comfort Zones

If you're not the boss at work, or self-employed and in charge of your own business, then you'll be the head of the household. To you, comfort means being in control of your own life, but you are also conventional about love and relationships, and you like to be in a twosome relationship where you both have your own careers and time to do your own thing. Socially you can play any role, from the barfly to the professional host, but there are times when you need to just snuggle up on the sofa alone listening to your favourite music.

Belonging, Family and Home

Family is important to you, and although it doesn't have to be the be-all of your life, you do crave security, support and a network of friends or colleagues who will be there for you just as much as you are there for them. You cherish your belongings, and material things do matter to you. Your home, your surroundings and your social status must all live up to your very high standards. Similarly, in a love relationship, you are attracted to those who can provide you with star status, or at least support you in your quest for your own.

The Moon's Lesson
You need to learn to take a less serious approach to life, and to not be so dependent on other people's opinions when your own are equally valid.

Tip to Boost Positive Lunar Energy
Be hedonistic rather than purely gymnastic. Opt for a balanced health regime: walk across mountains or wild landscapes, engage with your love of nature, but enjoy the pleasures of the flesh, too. On a Full Moon night, plant out a piece of white quartz in a pot or in your garden to bring you happiness in the lunar cycles to come.

Moon in Aquarius

Moods/Feelings
You are dispassionate, restrained, unruffled.

Sensitivity
You are cool and nonchalant.

Intuition
Your intuition is latent, indistinct, confused.

Moon Crystal: Amber
Around the Full Moon, a piece of amber kept in a pouch or in your pocket will ensure that your thinking remains clear and uncluttered when making any decisions.

Needs

Like Sagittarius, you don't seem to 'need' very much at all. In fact, things like feelings, moods, emotions and needs are the least of your worries when compared to thinking about the grander schemes of the planet or universe. Sure, you will analyse your mood, and you will discuss (and be very open about) everyone else's inadequacies and yearnings – but not your own. Why? Could it be that those darker regions of the mind are rather scary places, which you can't dissect, evaluate or judge with any objectivity? So, yes, you need space, freedom and the acceptance that you can be a little quirky and unfeeling; and yes, you need lovers or partners who give you time alone and the benefit of the doubt. You need a progressive, inventive lifestyle where feeling doesn't hold you back. Most of all, you need compassion, philosophical consideration, and warm hearts who don't judge you.

Reactions

Although you may be slow to react to other people's behaviour or moods, it's not because you don't notice or care. It's just that you would rather not involve yourself, fearing your own scepticism and lack of empathy might upset others. So, you stay detached and remote, even in the face of a new love interest who might be sending out shockwaves of desire for you! Rather like a brick wall, you can appear so hard to get close to that others back off; then you react by shrugging your shoulders and running.

Comfort Zones
You're happiest when you're exploring new ideas, buzzing with schemes for changing the world, or saving a near-extinct species. Rebelling against the norm, not living according to other people's expectations, and doing exactly the opposite of what someone suggests, all give you a sense of security, ease and optimism. You associate comfort not with cosy armchairs and roaring log fires, but with nurturing the grander machinations of the mind and the future of the universe, whether by engaging with nature, attending a lecture on quantum physics or becoming an astrologer.

Belonging, Family and Home
The Aquarian quest is to belong to humanity and experience some kind of connection to the universe. Aligning to the notion that All is One, your sense of belonging is no longer a personal condition, but a transpersonal one. Family is everywhere; globally, everyone is your friend, and there are no longer any boundaries set. In fact, it's hard for you to say you belong in any love relationship, let alone an exclusive, all-binding partnership. This radical approach can bring you a refreshing and exciting lifestyle, but it may create struggles with those who still view love as a one-to-one, exclusive, conditional experience.

The Moon's Lesson
Learn to accept that you have feelings like everybody else, and therefore they are universal.

Tip to Boost Positive Lunar Energy

During the Dark of the New Moon, get practical: declutter your home, clear out the attic, and make room for change, reformation and a fresh start. By doing so, you will also declutter your highly active mind and clear it out of all past stresses.

Moon in Pisces

Moods/Feelings

Your moods are fluctuating, overwhelming and ephemeral.

Sensitivity

Your sensitivity is radar-like, responsive and immediate.

Intuition

You have psychic intuition, but often confuse it with imagination.

Moon Crystal: Amethyst

Wear or carry amethyst to ensure that all love relationships remain stable and true to your desires, particularly during the Dark of the New Moon phase.

Needs

As the last sign of the zodiac, you are a Moon child who draws in all the moods, feelings and reactions of the other signs. Like a great psychic sponge, you are often swamped by the demands, fears, needs and emotions of other people, and it can be really hard to know which are your own. With your feelings adapting to those of someone else, you need to find a place within yourself where you know the truth of who you are. This is harder when you're younger, but as you get older, you will begin to see what you truly need, rather than what others may assume you lack. You need all-encompassing love. You need someone who holds and understands you, who allows you to be elusive if you must, but listens to your poetry or admires your canvas. You need to be able to come and go, to be the changeable, ineffable person that you are, without being judged or made to feel regret. You need to understand your needs, and that is the most important need of all.

Reactions

It is hard being a highly sensitive and reactive person in a world where there is constant energy, noise, pollution and geopathic stress all around you – not forgetting the negative and positive psychic energy exuding from everyone you meet, as well as the spiritual world. This can cause you to feel pulled in many directions, reacting to experiences and people without really knowing why. Although you adore large social events, parties and working in teams, sometimes the atmosphere can be overwhelming, and you need to retreat to a place of solitude.

Comfort Zones

In love relationships, you are most comfortable when few demands are placed on you and you're left to indulge in your imagination and artistic talents. The perfect holiday for you is to head to the hills, relax by the sea or commune with nature. Even though you often end up as the office 'agony aunt' or the boss's confidante, you prefer a low-key, harmonious, pressure-free work environment. If there's tension among colleagues, you escape to the loo or disappear to make the coffee.

Belonging, Family and Home

You desperately want to belong to something, but you're not sure what; you feel as if it must be something spiritual or unworldly, rather than the humdrum or ordinary aspects of life. Yes, you love your close family, but the world is a small place and you often find your feet in a more global or natural world community. The spiritual pull is strong, and you may find joining a belief group or religious body gives you a true sense of coming home that ordinary human bonding cannot fulfil. But once you share your soul with someone or something, you are locked into that for life.

The Moon's Lesson

You need to learn to create some barriers around the energies which flow so easily through you, whether through spiritual protection or magical empowerments. So, carry black tourmaline wherever you go to strengthen your emotional boundaries.

Tip to Boost Positive Lunar Energy

You see the beauty in most things, so create a sacred space where you can be at one with your lunar self. A personal sanctuary filled with familiars will empower you with charisma and give you a sense of your own identity.

Chapter 9

Moon Sign Goddesses and You

In Chapter Two we talked about how the Moon has long been associated with goddess energy. Here I will describe the Moon goddesses that you best connect with according to your astrological Moon sign, and those that will empower you with positive lunar energy.

In ancient Greek astrology, the Moon was associated with the goddess Selene, and in later Roman and medieval astrology, with Diana. (Both goddesses are renowned for their rather ambivalent nature, very much reflecting the Waxing and Waning phases of the Moon.) However, there are many goddesses associated with the Moon in world mythology, so here you will find a selection of twelve that correspond to the twelve signs of the zodiac.

In many cultures, the Moon was or is associated with male deities, but for the purposes of this book, using Western astrological methods, the lunar energy is associated with receptive, feminine energy, which is why I have used goddesses as opposed to gods.

The description of each goddess is followed by a simple ritual, petition or spell to enhance her attributes during the correct phase of the Moon. They will always be there to help you manifest your desires or intentions according to your Moon sign.

Moon Sign: Aries

Your Goddess: Bendis

Tradition: Thracian

The cult of Bendis flourished in Athens during the fifth century BCE. An ancient Thracian goddess of the Moon and hunting, and the consort of the Sun god, Sabazius, her festival was also associated with Artemis, and included competitive horse races and drunken orgies in the wild forests of Thrace. Known as the *Bendideia*, these nocturnal races were made up of teams of relay riders carrying lit torches, and were celebrated under the Full Moon.

Bendis is often depicted as accompanied by satyrs and the maenads, the wild, ecstatic followers of Dionysus. Her night time revelries are, like your Moon in Aries nature, extreme, daring and breathtakingly sensational.

ARIES MOON GODDESS RITUAL

To enhance your competitive spirit, feel free of ties, and take charge of your life, perform this ritual at a new crescent Moon.

You will need:

> a red candle
> red acrylic or watercolour paint
> paper or canvas (your choice)

1. Light the candle and sit or stand in front of it with your chosen art mediums. Now paint intuitively whatever you see before you in the candle flame, or just paint the candle and the flame. Whatever comes to you, whether wild and free strokes, or slow and careful lines, let yourself be taken out of yourself by the artist in you and free your spirit to the canvas/paper.

2. Keep your painting, however good or bad you believe it to be. During new crescent Moons, light a red candle and focus on your work of art, and the goddess will be with you when you need her.

Moon Sign: Taurus

Your Goddess: Áine

Tradition: Celtic

Often known in Irish folklore as the fairy queen, Áine was the Celtic goddess of love, fertility, the Moon, crops, farms and cattle. Responsible for the body's spirit and life-force, Áine is revered among Irish healers and she is still often invoked in spell work for well-being. She may have been known as the sweetheart of the *Sídhe* peoples, but she owned a standing stone, the Cathair Áine, which she possessively protected. If anyone sat on the stone, they would be in danger of temporarily losing their memory. If they sat on it three times, they would lose their memory forever. Like the Moon in Taurus nature, Áine is giving and loyal, and the natural pleasures of life keep her calm and sweet; but cross her, and she takes equal pleasure in revenge.

TAURUS MOON GODDESS RITUAL

To enhance your creative ability and improve your love relationships, perform this ritual during a Waxing Moon phase.

You will need:

> a large piece of white quartz
> a large piece of obsidian
> a large jar with a lid (glass or ceramic)
> 5 silver coins

1. Bless the crystals by holding them in your hands, one at a time, for one minute, closing your eyes and repeating: 'I bless this stone with love and peace, and all my self-belief for goodness to come.'
2. Place the two crystals in the jar, then drop in the coins, one at a time. Close the jar and say: 'Now blessed are the stones of protection, for me and all

creative ventures I now undertake. So mote it be, thank you Áine.'

3. Keep the jar in a secret place. When in need of further affirmation, hold the jar and repeat the enchantment to Áine.

Moon Sign: Gemini

Your Goddess: Britomartis

Tradition: Minoan

Britomartis was an ancient Cretan Moon goddess of the sea and possibly the inspiration for the Greek myth of Artemis. Her association with the Moon comes from a myth where she was pursued for nine months by King Minos. Her only escape route was to jump from a cliff into the sea, but she was caught in a fishing net and was transformed into the Moon in the sky. Although she was known as the 'good virgin', Minoan archaeological statues show a darker side of the goddess as a wild huntress accompanied by serpents and beasts. Similarly, the Moon in Gemini has two sides: civilised and logical, yet cold and often 'savage'.

GEMINI MOON GODDESS RITUAL

To enhance your natural ability to adapt to ever-changing circumstances and achieve success, perform this ritual at the Dark of the New Moon.

You will need:

> 2 pieces of yellow citrine
> a piece of blue lace agate
> 6 drops of clary sage essential oil

1. Place the three crystals in a line on your sacred table or altar, with the blue lace agate in the middle. Drop two drops of the essential oil on each crystal. As you do so, repeat the following charm:

> *'With oil of Clary break one in two,*
> *So both my wills are soon defined,*
> *So change is woven well in life,*
> *And citrine, agate, both are mine.'*

2. Place the stones in a pouch and carry it with you during the Dark of the New Moon to bring you success and the beneficial energy of Britomartis in the next lunar cycle.

Moon Sign: Cancer

Your Goddess: Selene

Tradition: Greek

Selene is sometimes known as the 'eye of the night', and she is symbolised as the Full Moon in the Wiccan Triple Moon Goddess sigil. Often depicted travelling across the night sky in her chariot, her myth tells of how she saw the mortal shepherd, Endymion, asleep in a cave and fell in love with him. Selene asked Zeus to send him into an eternal sleep so that he would stay forever young. She visited him every night and made love to him.

As a Full Moon goddess, Selene is associated with the colour white and is petitioned with white candles and roses. Like the Moon sign Cancer, she gives all of her love and yearns to be in harmony with the one she loves, but she often retreats into the night sky for fear of earthly reality.

CANCER MOON GODDESS RITUAL

To enhance your innate talent for cherishing others and to maximise the power of being loved in return, perform this ritual during the evening of the Full Moon.

You will need:

  a white candle
  a mirror, hanging on or leaning against a wall
  3 white roses

  1. Place the white candle in front of the mirror and light it. Pick up the roses one at a time and, before you place them down in front of the candle, kiss each rose and say: 'Selene, bring me

harmonious love and gentle kisses; thus forever my trust in you.'

2. When you have put down all three roses in a row in front of the candle, gaze at yourself and the flickering flame in the mirror for a few minutes. You may even glimpse Selene, but whatever the case, these moments of meditative calm will ensure the goddess will bring you the love you seek.

Moon Sign: Leo

Your Goddess: Inanna

Tradition: Mesopotamian

Inanna was the Babylonian goddess of the Moon, love, passion and sexuality. Accompanied by images of a crescent Moon, stars, lions and doves, she was the counterpart to Sumerian goddess Ishtar, who had an association with Venus, known as the Evening and Morning Star. The daughter of ancient Moon and Sun deities, Nanna and Ningal, Inanna means 'Queen Moon' or 'Lady Moon'. A hymn addresses her as the Moon Goddess and Morning Star when 'she made the night come forth like the moonlight'. She is one of the earliest deities to embody human character, reflecting the way the Moon in Leo person shines brightly and powerfully when they can be true to their dramatic self and live out their individuality and passion.

LEO MOON GODDESS RITUAL

To enhance your individual quest for being in the spotlight, perform this ritual at a new crescent Moon.

You will need:

> a warm bath
> a few drops of evening primrose oil (essential oil or bath essence)
> a few drops of almond oil (as above)
> 2 red candles
> a glass of champagne, sparkling wine or sparkling water

1. As you run your bath, add a few drops of evening primrose oil and almond oil to the water.
2. Light the candles and take your bath by candlelight. As you bathe, with glass in hand, say this enchantment to petition Inanna to always be there to boost your self-esteem and lead you into the spotlight: 'Inanna, Lady Moon, my spirit is strong, my desire is fervent, my need is passionate; please help me to be where I truly aim to be, the light shining brightly upon me for always.'
3. Enjoy the attention to come. Whenever you need a boost of Inanna power, dab a little evening primrose oil on your wrists and call her name.

Moon Sign: Virgo

Your Goddess: Losna

Tradition: Etruscan

Losna is most famously depicted on the back of an ancient mirror found in Praeneste (now Palestrina, near Rome). It shows a scene from the legend of Amukes (in Greek myth, King Amykos) a tyrannical king who killed everyone who challenged him in boxing matches, and his fight with Polekes or Pollux, the Argonaut who overcame him. Losna appears to be presiding over the fight between the two, a crescent Moon before her, symbolising her power to choose the true winner. Losna, a virgin goddess, controlled the tides and was concerned with purity and the rhythms of nature. Similarly, the Moon in Virgo defines and controls boundaries, purifies imbalance and has a talent for creating order out of chaos.

VIRGO MOON GODDESS RITUAL

To enhance your ability to categorise, organise and process the world around you for a happy lifestyle, perform this ritual during a Waning Moon.

You will need:

   3 white ribbons

a blue candle

a piece of moonstone or a piece of selenite

1. Wind each white ribbon around the candle. It doesn't matter if the ribbon drops down, it is the action that is important. As you do so, say:

'With ribbons white,
My Goddess light
Brings me happy days
Of calm and peaceful ways.'

2. Place the candle (without lighting it) on your altar or sacred table and place the moonstone or selenite in front of it. Leave in place until the next New Moon to promote Losna's attributes of balance and fairness.

Moon Sign: Libra

Your Goddess: Rhiannon

Tradition: Celtic (Welsh)

Rhiannon is the Welsh Moon goddess of birds, fertility, enchantment, charms and poetic incantations. Rhiannon was born at the first ever Moon rise and manifests as a beautiful lady riding a pale horse, surrounded by larks, her favoured songbirds. The larks can wake spirits or send mortals to sleep, and Rhiannon bestows grace and aesthetic talent on those who worship her. In one myth, accused of devouring her own child, Rhiannon is eventually redeemed and has thus become associated with truth and justice. Rhiannon's lunar charm mimics the Moon in Libra person's need for fair play and appreciation of sophistication and beauty in life.

LIBRA MOON GODDESS RITUAL

To enhance and boost your own aesthetic principles and help you achieve personal success, start this ritual during a new crescent Moon and finish by the Dark of the New Moon.

You will need:

a firm A4/A3 pinboard or wooden panel
a collection of images cut out from magazines or
    printed off from the internet – they must include
    birds, horses and anything you find 'beautiful'

1. Create a beautiful mood board by arranging the images on your pinboard or wooden panel. Including Rhiannon's favoured creatures will harness her power to invoke creative ideas and all the imagination you need to be a success. As you set up your mood board, thank Rhiannon for her blessing. You can take as long as you like, but finish before the next Dark of the New Moon.

2. Once the mood board is finished, leave it somewhere centre stage in your home to remind you daily of your talents. Call on the goddess whenever you need creative back-up.

Moon Sign: Scorpio

Your Goddess: Lilith

Tradition: Sumerian/Hebrew

Long before Lilith was associated with demonic sexuality in Hebrew mythology, she was the handmaiden to the Sumerian goddess Inanna. Known as 'Lilitu', she was a winged woman or bird and a New Moon goddess. In Jewish lore, Lilith was denounced as a succubus who visited lonely men on the night of a New Moon, seducing them to impregnate her with demon children. She later became the archetypal femme fatale and a figure of female sexuality in Western patriarchal society. As the Moon goddess who represents the dark phase of the Moon, Lilith champions the Moon in Scorpio characteristics of independence, passion and sexuality in the most positive sense.

SCORPIO MOON GODDESS RITUAL

To enhance your mysterious powers and your ability to cut through illusions to discover the truth, perform this during the Dark of the New Moon.

You will need:

a small piece of paper and a pen
a piece of black obsidian or onyx
a small box with a lid

1. On the piece of paper, write down the following petition to Lilith:

    'My sexuality is sacred as the Moon is you,
    My pleasure yours, and all is true,
    Lilith bring me wisdom, dark and light,
    To see through those who choose the night.'

2. Wrap the paper around the stone and place it in the box. Put the box in a secret place and leave it there until the next Dark of the New Moon. Take out the paper and stone and repeat the charm each month to boost your power, enabling you to see the truth of any matter and enhancing any personal quest.

Moon Sign: Sagittarius

Your Goddess: Artemis

Tradition: Greek

The twin sister of Apollo, Artemis was revered as the goddess of the hunt, childbirth, wild animals and the Moon. Represented by the Waxing Moon in the Triple

Goddess tradition, she is the embodiment of exploration and the sacredness of individuality. Her only true love was her companion, the hunter Orion. As a devout virginal goddess, those who transgressed her vows were usually punished, such as Actaeon who was turned into a stag as punishment for seeing her bathing naked.

Artemis is usually depicted with a bow and arrow, a Waxing crescent Moon and deer. Like Artemis, the Moon in Sagittarius character is fiercely self-willed, yet will rise to defend those that it truly cares for.

SAGITTARIUS MOON GODDESS RITUAL

To enhance Artemis's self-determination and willpower, and to manifest your desires, perform this ritual during a Waxing Moon.

You will need:

> 3 green candles
> 1 green leaf (or an image of the same)
> 1 yellow flower (or an image of the same)
> 1 blue flower (or an image of the same)

1. Light the candles on your altar or sacred table. Place the leaf in front of one candle and a flower in front of each of the others. As you do so, repeat the following enchantment:

'With green, then blue and yellow hue,
All nature sings to Artemis's tune
Desires unfold and fire my quest
To bring my best to manifest.'

2. Leave in place in your sacred space until the Full
    Moon to seal your intention to Artemis. Repeat
    as necessary.

Moon Sign: Capricorn

Your Goddess: Hecate

Tradition: Greek

In traditional lore, Hecate represents the Waning Moon in
the Triple Moon Goddess. Ruling the Greek underworld,
Hecate was accompanied by wild dogs and serpents, and
was usually depicted carrying a burning torch. She was
associated with crossroads, doorways and sorcery. As a
lunar deity, she was propitiated during the Deipnon, a
festive meal held to honour her entourage of restless spirits during the Dark of the New Moon. Hecate's ancient
wisdom is at the heart of the Moon in Capricorn psyche.
You have a deep well of knowledge at your disposal, and
this spell will help you to unleash that wisdom.

CAPRICORN MOON GODDESS RITUAL

To enhance inner wisdom and outer success, perform this ritual during a Dark of the New Moon phase.

You will need:

>   an image of a crossroads – you can simply draw a
>   crossroads on a piece of paper
>   a piece of moonstone
>   a piece of white quartz
>   sandalwood incense

1. Place the image on your altar or sacred table. Position the two crystals at the crossroads point of the image.
2. Light the incense and close your eyes. For a moment, focus on your own inner wisdom and how it can bring you outer success. Finally, gaze at the crystals as you repeat:

> *'By moonstone bright,*
> *By white quartz true,*
> *My inner wisdom will be ensured,*
> *Success and progress, both fulfilled.*
> *Thank you, Hecate, for this night,*
> *And bring me answers bold and bright.'*

3. Extinguish the incense when you've finished your spell, but leave the petition overnight to draw

down the power of Hecate's New Moon. Call on her or repeat the spell if you need to boost your chances of success.

Moon Sign: Aquarius

Your Goddess: Arianrhod

Tradition: Celtic (Welsh)

Sister to the Celtic trickster, Gwydion, Arianrhod was known as 'The Silver Wheel' and worshipped as a Full Moon goddess. She represents the element of Air, self-assurance, logical thought and karma. Her palace in the sky was known as Caer Arianrhod (the constellation Corona Borealis). This mirrored her legendary submerged castle, where she lived a wanton life gallivanting with mermen, yet casting astute magic spells. Her 'Silver Wheel' carried dead warriors to her starry palace, which was also thought to be a portal between worlds.

Moon in Aquarius people are similar to the free-spirited Arianrhod: not prepared to bend to anyone's expectations, staunchly independent and able to see beyond the veil to a wider perspective of life and the universe .

AQUARIUS MOON GODDESS RITUAL

To enhance your individuality and develop your incredible foresight, perform this spell for Arianrhod during a Full Moon.

You will need:

> an orange candle
> an image of a spoked wheel, or the Wheel of
>   Fortune tarot card
> a piece of Amber

1. Light the candle on your altar or sacred table and place the card or image in front of it, face up. Place your piece of amber on the card and focus for a while on the candle flame.
2. Pick up the amber and hold it close to the flame (close enough to feel the warmth, but not so close as to feel hot). Now say this charm:

> *'With this stone I give my faith,*
> *With this stone you bring me grace,*
> *And all that is will be a tune,*
> *To sing beneath the fullest Moon,*
> *A song of love and giving time,*
> *For every moment thine and mine.'*

3. Focus for a few moments on your petition, then blow out the candle and replace the stone on the

image or card. Leave in place during the Full Moon to align the goddess's power to you. Repeat as needed.

Moon Sign: Pisces

Your Goddess: Cerridwen

Tradition: Celtic (Welsh)

Associated with the Waning Moon, Cerridwen's magical inspiration came from her large cauldron of elixir called *awen*, meaning both divine spirit and poetic inspiration. Stirring this magical brew for a year to yield just three precious drops, anyone who drank the elixir would be bestowed with the wisdom of the past, the knowledge of the present, and the secrets of the future.

Cerridwen represents magic, inspiration, art and poetry. As a shapeshifter, she has the power to transform herself into any creature or being she desires. Similarly, Moon in Pisces people often take on the identity of the one they are with, or are able to act a part that hides their true self. Take the time to find your own authenticity.

PISCES MOON GODDESS RITUAL

To enhance your sense of identity and to feel liberated from the power of others, perform this ritual during a Waning Moon.

You will need:

a white candle

a bowl, cauldron or chalice filled with spring or
mineral water

a handful of white rose petals, lavender petals
and basil leaves

3 drops of lemon essential oil

3 drops of jasmine essential oil

3 drops of nutmeg essential oil

1. Light the candle on your altar or sacred table on
   the evening of a Waning Moon, and place it behind
   the chalice filled with water.

2. Sprinkle the petals and leaves on to the surface
   of the water and focus on who you really are, and
   how you want others to see you.

3. Drop three drops of each of the essential oils into
   the bowl. Dip your finger into the liquid and stir
   once round clockwise, and once anticlockwise.
   Finally, touch your damp finger to the middle of
   your forehead (the Crown Chakra) and hold it
   there as you say: 'I anoint myself with the magic of
   awen, to find my true self among all others. Thank
   you, Cerridwen, for your blessing.'

4. Leave the sacred bowl in place until the new
   crescent Moon to revitalise your inner sense of
   individuality, and call on Cerridwen for her blessing whenever you feel in need of a boost to your
   sense of ego.

Chapter 10

Self-protection Grids for Your Moon Sign

We all need protection from outside negativity, whether that's other people's difficult psychic energy or geopathic stress (see page 141). The Moon is a body of protection, security and homeliness, so it's right to draw down her powers to wrap you in a positive aura and cocoon you and your family.

Don't worry if you have a family of radically different Moon signs; work with your own Moon sign and no other. If you are an Aries Moon, for example, it doesn't matter if your partner is a Taurus and your children are a range of other Moon signs. It is you who is performing the ritual, and therefore it is your Moon which is the potent force that will create and be the recipient of the protective shield for you all.

What is a Grid?

For each Moon sign, there is a specific crystal placement grid to protect your home from negativity. Grids are simply a way of combining and reinforcing the energy of crystals, which resonate to specific symbolic patterns in the universe. This is often known as sacred geometry.

When to Perform Your Grid

Perform your grid during the phase of the Moon under which you were born (see page 184).

For example, if you're an Aries Moon born during the Full Moon phase, perform the Aries grid ritual during any Full Moon phase. If you're a Capricorn Moon born during the Waning Moon, perform during any Waning Moon phase, and so on.

You can either leave the grid permanently in place if you have the space, or you can reinforce the energy either once a month, or whenever you feel necessary, by repeating the ritual. Remember, though, that best results are achieved if you create the grid during your own natal Moon phase. If the ritual asks you to leave it for one lunar cycle to reinforce the energy, then do so.

ARIES MOON PROTECTION GRID

With your fiery Moon, you may feel that you don't need much protection, as you're so driven and adventurous. However, we are all vulnerable to negativity. Perform this grid ritual in a south corner of your home.

You will need:

>6 pieces of carnelian
>a piece of paper and pen (if required)
>a red candle

1. Lay the crystals out in a six-pointed star shape. You may find it helpful to draw an illustration of a six-pointed star and place the crystals on its points. The easiest way to get accurate points without drawing a star is to lay three crystals in an equal triangle with one point facing north, and then lay the remaining three crystals as a triangle over the first with one point facing south.
2. Place the red candle in the middle of the star and light it. Repeat the following affirmation: 'With six red stones, my home is safe and all my family too. Thank you, Moon, for protecting me from this night.'
3. Blow out the candle when you are ready and leave the grid for at least two more nights to charge your home with positive lunar energy.

TAURUS MOON PROTECTION GRID

As a Taurus Moon person, you're astute about how much security you need, and make these measures clear to would-be trespassers with a plethora of locks or alarms. However, you can benefit from this protection grid to ensure your home is safe from invisible energies, too.

You will need:

> 3 × 1-metre (3-foot) lengths of blue ribbon
> sandalwood essential oil
> 3 sprigs of lavender
> 3 sprigs of parsley

1. Tie the three blue ribbons together at one end, then plait together the rest of their lengths and tie off at the end. Make three further knots, equally spaced, along the length of the plait.
2. Sprinkle drops of sandalwood essential oil along the length of ribbon and then insert a sprig each of lavender and parsley into each of the three central knots.
3. Hang the braid on a wall or the edge of a mirror, or place it on a ledge. The important thing is that it should be facing your front entrance door. As you do so, repeat:

> *'Bless this house with my lunar light,*
> *for always protected in our sight.'*

4. When hung in the hallway facing your entrance door, this magical braid will protect you from all incoming negativity.

GEMINI MOON PROTECTION GRID

As a Gemini, they say you're as scatty in your home as you are in your feelings, which is why you need some stabilising energy around you. This Gemini Moon grid will also keep you safe from the psychic negativity of others.

You will need:

3 pieces of citrine
3 yellow candles
ground cinnamon
a small box or pouch

1. In an east corner of your home, arrange the citrine pieces in a triangle and position the three yellow candles at each point.
2. Light the candles, relax and then anoint the grid by sprinkling pinches of cinnamon on to the candle flames and the crystals. As you do so, repeat this affirmation:

   'With crystals blessed my home is fine,
   This grid will keep me safe for all time.'

3. When you are ready, blow out the candles and leave the grid in place for one lunar cycle. After this, place the citrine in the box or pouch and keep it in the east corner of your home to attract beneficial energy.

CANCER MOON PROTECTION GRID

Your home is a very special comfort zone, and, like any fortress, you want maximum security. When placed by your main entrance door, this special yet highly discreet grid will keep you safe from all.

You will need:

> 5 tiny moonstones
> 5 tiny pink tourmaline polished stones
> a piece of onyx or obsidian
> a sage smudging stick

1. Arrange the moonstones in a small circle near your main entrance door, then arrange the tourmaline stones in an outer circle around the moonstones. In the centre, place the black stone.
2. Light the smudging stick and walk through all areas or rooms of your house with it. As you do so, use the smudging stick to trace an imaginary circle in the air at each threshold and repeat: 'With these crystals, all negativity be gone, and my home protected for always.'
3. Return to your stone circle and extinguish the smudging stick. Leave the crystals in place for at least one lunar cycle to maximise the grid's protective powers.

LEO MOON PROTECTION GRID

Bursting with creative energy, it's likely your home is filled with cherished possessions and beautiful things. To protect not only you and your family, but also your personal richness of spirit, place this grid 'outside' the home for maximum results.

You will need:

a piece of paper and a pen (if needed)
5 pieces of black tourmaline
1 piece of white quartz

1. This grid uses the method of 'earth acupuncture', or, in other words, burying crystals in the ground. If you do not have a garden, you can replicate this symbolically by drawing a rough illustration of your home sitting in the middle of a circle.
2. Now either bury the five black crystals, equally spaced, in a circle around your house, or if you're working with an image, place the crystals on the paper in a circle.
3. Put the white quartz either in the core of your home, right at its epicentre, or in the middle of the drawn image.
4. Repeat:

   'With these five crystals under moonlight true,
   My home is protected and safe for us too.

With this white quartz inside my circle complete,
From the power of the Moon I can safely retreat.'

5.   If you illustrated the image, keep it in a safe place
     in the centre of your home. If you buried the crys-
     tals in the garden, simply keep the white quartz in
     its special central place to enable the grid to work
     its magic ring of protection.

Virgo Moon Protection Grid

I know you like a neat and tidy place, but this grid won't
add any extra clutter, nor will it get in your way. To protect your space, all you need is this simple knotted grid,
placed discreetly in a bedroom drawer or under your bed
(it definitely needs to be in your bedroom).

You will need:

a 1-metre (3-foot) length of black ribbon
a 1-metre (3-foot) length of white ribbon
a 1-metre (3-foot) length of red ribbon
5 dried bay leaves

1.   First knot together the three ribbons at one end.
     Plait the ribbons together and tie off at the other
     end with another knot. Next make three more
     knots, equally spaced along the length of the braid.
2.   Insert a bay leaf into each knot.

3. Place the finished knot grid into your chosen safe
    place in the bedroom. To seal your petition to the
    Moon, say:

    'With woven ribbons black to banish,
    With red ones too my foes to vanquish,
    White exiles bad, but casts no harm,
    For I am safe when said this charm.'

4. Leave in place for at least one lunar cycle, and
    repeat the charm if desired.

LIBRA MOON PROTECTION GRID

You're renowned for a perfectly lovely looking home, so this
simple illustrated grid will not only enhance aesthetic pleasure,
but also keep you safe from any unwanted negative energy.

You will need:

    a gold candle
    a silver candle
    a pen and a piece of paper
    6 small mahogany obsidian stones
    1 small piece of white quartz

1. Light the candles on your altar or sacred table.
    Place the silver candle to the right of your working
    area and the gold to the left.

2. On the piece of paper, draw a six-pointed star. (The easiest way to do this is to draw two equal-sided triangles, the first with the first point facing north, the second crossing the first with the first point facing south.)

3. Place the six obsidian stones on each point of the star, and the white quartz in the centre. Call on the Moon to bring you peace and harmony by saying:

   'This star is filled with crystals fine,
   My home is safe and all will shine.'

4. Let the candles burn for a few minutes to invite the energy into your home, then blow them out. Leave the grid until the day of next Full Moon, then keep the crystals in a safe place until you want to reinforce the harmonious energy again.

SCORPIO MOON PROTECTION GRID

Discreet but quietly controlling, it's rare for you to let yourself become vulnerable to outside negativity and your home is your fortress. Place this grid in a permanent spot in the north part of your home to guard your self-confident determination and protect your family.

You will need:

a white candle

3 pieces of black tourmaline or onyx
a small glass jar with lid or stopper
a few drops of clove essential oil
a few drops of ginger essential oil
a black ribbon

1. Light the candle and assemble your ingredients
    in front of you. First put the crystals into the jar,
    then add a few drops of each oil to the jar. As you
    do so, say:

    'This jar is filled with love and protection
    To bring me harmony and positive connection.'

2. Seal the jar and tie the black ribbon around it.
    Place in a north corner of your home to enhance
    all positive aspects of your home life.

SAGITTARIUS MOON PROTECTION GRID

Unless you have a very homely Sun sign (star sign) such
as Taurus or Cancer, the chances are you're out on your
travels most of the time. But you still need a base, and your
own kind of 'home comforts', so this crystal grid will keep
you grounded and safe from negativity.

You will need:

a white candle

3 pieces of turquoise
a piece of raffia, or white ribbon
3 drops of tea tree essential oil
3 drops of lemon verbena essential oil

1. Light the candle and hold the crystals in your hands as you say: 'Thank you, Moon, for these stones to bring me luck and safety, whether at home or on my travels.'
2. Anoint each of the stones with one drop of each of the oils, then place them in a triangle on a table or ledge by your main entrance. Wind the twine or ribbon around and around the three crystals in a spiralling or circular way to absorb the oils.
3. This grid will bring you happy home days, and good luck on your travels. Touch the stones each time you go in or out for extra goodness.

CAPRICORN MOON PROTECTION GRID

When placed in the northwest corner of your home, this empowering crystal grid will bring you success in all ventures, as well as protection from other people's negative vibes.

You will need:

a space big enough to set up your grid
a black candle

    a white quartz amplifier stone (one that is quite
      large or pointed)
    a collection of tumbled stones of any of the
      following: onyx, black tourmaline, jade, moss
      agate, malachite

1. Decide how much space you will need, as this is a grid that you can make as large or as small as you require. It is going to take the form of a spiral.
2. Light the candle and start by placing the white quartz in the centre in front of the candle. Gradually begin to arrange the tumbled stones in a spiral around it, building it in an anticlockwise direction and keeping the stones aligned closely together.
3. When you have finished, gaze into the candle flame and say: 'This lunar spiral brings me success in all at home and for the best.'
4. Blow out the candle when you are ready. Leave the grid in place for at least one lunar cycle from when you first perform the ritual. You can also change the order of your stones to maximise their resonance to the Moon.

AQUARIUS MOON PROTECTION GRID

To inspire you with creativity in the home and to protect your loved ones, place this grid in a western corner of your home.

You will need:

a white candle
5 small pieces of white quartz
10 small turquoise polished stones
4 small, equal-sized pieces of amber

1. First, place the candle somewhere where you can leave the grid set up for at least one lunar cycle from when you perform the ritual.
2. Take the five pieces of white quartz and place them in a circle around the candle. Next, take the turquoise stones and place them in a larger circle surrounding the white quartz circle, making sure to leave enough space between the two circles to place the amber. Finally, place the four amber pieces between the two circles at the four compass points, one to the north, one to the south, one to the east and one to the west.
3. Finally light the candle, thank the Moon for bringing you positive energy, and focus on the flame for a few minutes to seal your intention. Blow out the candle when you are ready, and leave the grid in place as described above.

PISCES MOON PROTECTION GRID

To ensure you are spiritually in harmony with your surroundings and protected from negative psychic energy, place this grid in the centre of your home and leave for at least one lunar cycle from when you perform this ritual.

You will need:

> 2 blue candles
> a pen and piece of paper
> a large blue lace agate crystal
> 8 vintage or skeleton-type door keys (try finding these in a junk shop; alternatively you can use images of the same), to represent the locking out of all negative energy

1. First light the candles, and place one to the left of your intended grid, and one to the right.
2. Draw the points of a compass on the paper: a line from north to south, a line crossing from east to west, then one from northwest to southeast and one from northeast to southwest. This will give you eight compass points in total. They don't have to be exactly equidistant.
3. Place the blue lace agate crystal in the centre of the paper and position the keys along each of the lines, with the teeth of each key pointing towards the compass point. As you position each key, say: 'With these keys I lock out all negativity from my life and home.'
4. Leave in place for one complete lunar cycle from the day you perform the grid, and repeat as necessary.

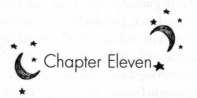

Chapter Eleven

Black Moon Lilith and Self-empowerment

Finally, we come to the shadowy side of the Moon's influence; the mysterious, invisible phase of the Moon's cycle, when she is furthest away from the Earth. Here we are truly at the darkest side or edge of the Moon. With this knowledge, we can learn how to illuminate our souls and heal our lives by working with our true sexual energy flow, unique to us.

Bringing the dark to light empowers our authentic self, enabling us to express our personal desires and cut through our defences and illusions.

The Dark Goddess and Lilith

The 'Dark Goddess' archetype is associated with sex, transformation, resurrection, magic, the occult and the taboo. There are many goddesses associated with this aspect of the Moon, such as Kali, Hecate, Circe, and Kybele, but one of the most notorious is Lilith.

Originally a handmaiden to the goddess Inanna (see

page 241), Lilith guided people to Inanna's sacred temple for sexual rites. Later, patriarchal religion described her as Adam's first wife, who, rather than subjugate herself to his masculine will, defied him and refused to have sex with him, preferring exile. She later became known as a terrifying demon in Hebrew mythology. By the nineteenth century, Lilith's association with the liberated female cast her in the role of the archetypal femme fatale.

Black Moon Lilith in Astrology

In astrology, Black Moon Lilith represents our deepest desires, and how to reclaim a true sense of sexual individuality.

Lilith appears in three astrological roles. One is the asteroid Lilith. In astrology, this reflects themes of rejection and/or flight in our lives.

She is also associated with the hypothetical 'Dark Moon', a controversial satellite apparently orbiting the Earth, but as yet undiscovered. In astrology, the Dark Moon reflects our pain, or fear of our deep desire.

But we are going to work with 'Black Moon Lilith', which reveals your secret sexuality and how to live it out, releasing you from other people's expectations or assumptions and your own illusions.

So, when you consult the internet or ephemeris, please remember you are working with Black Moon Lilith, not the other two described above.

Black Moon Lilith Facts

The astrological glyph used for Black Moon Lilith is an inverted black crescent Moon underpinned by a black cross.

Black Moon Lilith is an invisible energy vortex, a point in space known as the lunar apogee (in other words, the point when the Moon is furthest away from Earth).

As the Moon moves further away from the Earth in her erratic elliptical orbit, she eventually conjuncts this 'invisible point' in space. When she is closest to the Earth (the lunar perigee), Black Moon Lilith will then be opposite the Moon.

It takes just under nine years for Black Moon Lilith to travel around the zodiac.

In astrology, there are two calculations for the path of the Black Moon Lilith, known as the 'Mean' and the 'True'.

When checking out which sign your Black Moon Lilith is in, you may find both calculations listed in the ephemeris. Generally, most astrologers use the Mean calculation. The difference of twelve degrees between the two can affect the position when near the cusp, but the Mean calculation is usually thought to be more accurate. So, if you find your Mean Black Moon Lilith is very close to the end or beginning of a sign, check out

the next-door sign's description, too, to see which
you instinctively feel fits.

Symbol and Meaning

As a lady of the night, Black Moon Lilith is seen as a shadow
reflection of the Moon, associated with the dark feminine archetype. Lilith's astrological associations include
self-empowerment, freedom, independence, darkness,
temptation, bewitchment, defiance and ambiguity.

This power point placement in our birth chart represents those shadowy things hidden within us that need to
be released and understood. These include our vulnerable
side (the dark truth of ourselves), our sexual arousals and
fantasies, and our instincts: the deep truths of our psyche.

However, Dark Moon Lilith, when her energy is understood, can help empower you, heal you and even bring out
the sex goddess in you. As an inner temptress, she can also
go too far and create disharmony in your relationships.
Knowing which buttons might get pushed, and why, can
help you navigate this dark side of your lunar landscape.

To discover where Black Moon Lilith lies in your chart,
go to one of the websites listed on page 289.

Next, look through the following Black Moon Lilith
placements to understand your hidden sexual potency, and
to perform a ritual to empower you and regain your true
authentic sexual self.

Black Moon Lilith in Aries

Sexual Expression

The hunt and sexual conquest turn you on just as much as all the steamy action. In fact, if you're ignored or rejected, you become even more determined to get your way. You thrive on challenging, adrenaline-charged sex, with people who are equally hot-headed, impulsive and potent. You're looking for someone who accepts that you need to be first in everything, whether it's first in the shower, or the first to win a game of strip poker. When you say you want sex now, you mean now, not later.

Shadow Side

Competitive and a tad selfish in bed, you need constant reassurance that you are the best sexual partner, or the 'fairest of them all'. Deep down, you have a fragile ego, which is why you compensate by being a show-off and often not having time to commit yourself to anyone.

Empowerment Ritual

This will help you to manage your self-centred temperamental side and to cool your lusty ardour. During a Waxing Moon cycle, sprinkle a few drops of lavender essential oil on three pink tourmaline crystals and place them in the shape of a triangle in a west corner of your home. Leave for one lunar cycle to empower you with compassion for yourself, and others too.

Black Moon Lilith in Taurus

Sexual Expression
You take a very down-to-earth approach to sex, and are a generous, sensitive and understanding lover. You see lovemaking as an art form and adore making your partner happy. Being straightforward about sex is a bonus because you know exactly what you want and you're not afraid to ask for it. Quality sex is more important than anything else. Self-indulgent, your lust for love, luxury and money can be an aphrodisiac for others.

Shadow Side
Your jealousy can create tension in love relationships, and it can make you seem overly possessive, particularly about money or your lover. Accept that you need to work hard to make love work and not let your desires take over from reality.

Empowerment Ritual
This will help you understand your deeper passions and develop your creative talents. During a Full Moon, place five garnets in a circle on the table closest to your front door. This will boost your self-esteem every time you walk past. Leave in place for one lunar cycle from when you perform this ritual, adding a piece of white quartz to the centre during the Dark of the New Moon.

Black Moon Lilith in Gemini

Sexual Expression
Playful, capricious and unreliable, you love erotic phone calls and unpredictable sex. You often move from lover to lover in your search for someone to satisfy your restless spirit. Your light and breezy approach to sex is often misunderstood, and you believe physical intimacy is the key to being loved and finding a soulmate. Ironically, what you need to discover is that the perfect love is deep within yourself.

Shadow Side
You can be devious, and may take a shine to your best friend's lover or become flirtatious just to get attention. Playing this capricious role also saves you from making any commitment or getting serious about anyone who makes you feel vulnerable. Accept that you have great charm, but it is simply a mask for your fear of someone seeing your dark side.

Empowerment Ritual
Just after the Dark of the New Moon phase, light two yellow candles and place five small pieces of citrine in front of them. Leave for five minutes while you focus on understanding your deeper motives. Blow out the candles, put the crystals in a pouch, and carry it with you on every social occasion for one lunar cycle to empower you with a sense of focus and dedication to your complex psyche.

Black Moon Lilith in Cancer

Sexual Expression

Sensitive, intuitive and nurturing, you're renowned for attracting people to you without really trying. But that cautious, cool outer shell hides a highly sexual and sensual lover inside. You're often frustrated, sexually and emotionally, because you fear being rejected if you ask for what turns you on. Contradictorily, you want to belong to someone, but hate being possessed. When you finally commit and let go of your doubts and fears, however, you are the most loyal and loving sex partner.

Shadow Side

You can be either clingy or totally aloof. These changing moods reflect your need for constant reassurance and your fear of rejection. You hate emotional dramas and the idea of separation, yet, ironically, you attract unreliable partners to you. Accept that you need stability, and trust that you can form a stable, secure relationship with one other.

Empowerment Ritual

This will fill you with genuine self-love so that others can love you better. On a Full Moon night, place three pieces of amethyst in a triangle shape in a north corner of your home. Leave them in place for one lunar cycle.

Black Moon Lilith in Leo

Sexual Expression

You insist on being number one in any love relationship, and you fan the flames of sexual desire for as long as possible. Vain, flamboyant and theatrical, you love to put on a show or act a part, and sometimes you don't know who you really are. Never short of admirers, you exude unlimited passion and a flamboyant sexuality. Luxury, fame and all the glitz make you feel loved. But beneath the flashy exterior, you have a soft heart.

Shadow Side

You can be totally self-absorbed, wanting only what's great for you and always thinking that you're right and everyone else is wrong. You appear to not care what people say, when in fact you secretly doubt your own power and are acutely sensitive to criticism. Realise that yes, you deserve love, but don't resort to ruthless means to get it. Be honest about who you are to create a real affinity with someone.

Empowerment Ritual

This will help you value yourself and release you from self-doubt. Light two white candles in front of a mirror every Full Moon and say: 'I deserve love just by virtue of being on this planet, and I am in touch with the lunar light.'

Black Moon Lilith in Virgo

Sexual Expression

Witty and kind, but highly sensitive, you need an intellectual basis for a love relationship rather than just physical desire. It takes a long time until you're confident enough to reveal your own sexual needs, even though you can appear to be quite an authority on sex. The more knowledge you acquire, whether you read it, dream it or simply do it, the better a sex guru you become. Delicacy, discretion and discernment ignite your sexual appetite, not raw lust.

Shadow Side

With your fear of disorder and imperfection, things like love, anger, jealousy and sentimentality are treated like bits of clutter to be kept hidden in the laundry bin. But you need to take them out and wash them squeaky clean. Realise that you do have sexual feelings, and that denying them only makes you obsessive and nit-picking.

Empowerment Ritual

This will liberate you from mistrust, and help you to free yourself from sexual inhibitions. On the night of the Full Moon, place one piece of red carnelian beneath your pillow, and another on a window ledge exposed to the moonlight (even if it's cloudy). Leave in place for one lunar cycle.

Black Moon Lilith in Libra

Sexual Expression

Seductive and sophisticated, you are also a paradoxical lover. Always polite and ready to sexually please, you're a hopeless romantic. However, hopeless romantics have one big problem: there might just be someone more beautiful and perfect round the next corner. You may yearn for the deepest, most passionate love affair, but you often reject the 'right one' in your search for an ideal that doesn't exist.

Shadow Side

Because you're an approval-seeker, you find it hard to say 'no'. You believe that if someone adores you, all you have to do is say 'yes' and the dream will come true. But when it doesn't, which is most of the time, you feel let down and can turn the tables by becoming sexually selective and difficult to please.

Empowerment Ritual

This will help you to accept that you are only human, and no one is divine. During the Waxing Moon, gather a collection of pebbles and crystals (of your choice), along with twigs, sprigs, dried flowers, leaves: anything foraged from nature. Place these in a jar, cover with the lid and tie with a black ribbon. Leave for one lunar cycle to empower you with self-worth.

Black Moon Lilith in Scorpio

Sexual Expression
Serious about life and love, and unconsciously cultivating an aura of mystery, your charismatic sexuality draws others to you to invoke intense, compelling and sometimes bittersweet love affairs. In fact, what you desire is an utter merging of bodies, to reconnect to your sacred sexual self, or surrender to the cosmos. 'Sin-sational', demanding and physically insatiable, when you're truly in love, you'll move mountains to be at your lover's side.

Shadow Side
Manipulative, suspicious and dangerously attractive, you can turn love into extreme hatred if you're ever betrayed; that's when your vengeful nature becomes the cruellest sting in the tail. Lilith's curse gives you double standards: you may indulge in the drama of a clandestine affair, knowing you can't trust anyone, not even yourself.

Empowerment Ritual
This will align you to the true integrity of your soul and release you from mistrust. During the Full Moon, light a red candle and place five black tourmaline crystals in the shape of a pentacle before it. Gaze into the flame and repeat: 'My jealousy is only a reaction to a fear of rejection. My need to manipulate is really a need to feel I am not powerless. I am powerful and humble too.' Blow out the candle and leave for one lunar cycle.

Black Moon Lilith in Sagittarius

Sexual Expression
Independent and hilarious, you just want to celebrate life through sexy interaction. You value sexual freedom. Your insatiable appetite for romance and crazy fun-loving attitude make you highly desirable, but you can be totally unreliable. A wild rover, you're passionate about flirting with passing strangers, and sex must be a liberating, explorative or simply spontaneous experience.

Shadow Side
Yes, you need to roam, whether in your head or to many different beds. That's why the act of making a promise to one person can bring out your vulnerable side, leading you to accuse your lover of being too possessive or demanding. In fact, you live in a complete romantic fantasy world. A commitment brings a terrifying sense of finality for you, because it reminds you that you're not immortal.

Empowerment Ritual
To manage and understand your dark side, make a commitment to light a white candle and honour your individuality *every* Full Moon. When you next enter into a relationship with someone, light a second candle alongside your own, and honour their individual needs too. Tough, but liberating.

Black Moon Lilith in Capricorn

Sexual Expression

The bonding and loving power of sexual pleasure is far more important to you than sex for the sake of sex. Sensual but aloof, you're not exactly a tiger on the rampage when you first meet a lover. But behind that polished image, you have a high sex drive and can be passion personified when someone melts your icy defences. A bit of a control freak in the office (ruthlessly) and in bed (nicely), power and prestige are also part of what motivates your sexual desire.

Shadow Side

You have a blinkered perception of what you believe is 'right' in a relationship. The last thing you want is a partner who's the life and soul of every other party except yours. Learn to let go and trust a little, and once you accept that not everyone is as controlling as you, you can get down to the serious business of long-term partnership.

Empowerment Ritual

This will enable you to understand that power isn't the only thing in love and life, and that you can be empowered by other means. Perform this ritual during the Dark of the New Moon. Take three pieces of white quartz and make a large triangle, big enough to put your hand in the middle of the space. Do so and repeat: 'Here, in this space, is universal empowerment for me, no longer power and control to defend myself, so mote it be.'

Perform every New Moon until you feel released.

Black Moon Lilith in Aquarius

Sexual Expression
Sexually broad-minded, liberated and experimental, you're actually inhibited about merging in some deeper spiritual or emotional sexual union. With a desire to shock and to prove you're utterly different, you may prefer lovers who are totally radical in looks or gender, or unacceptable to your culture. Even though you don't want to be committed to the same sexual partner for life, you will always remain a true friend to anyone who's been in an intimate relationship with you.

Shadow Side
When you feel threatened by the chains of commitment, your defences rise as rebel and anarchist. You accuse others of being overly emotional, demanding too much and tying you down. Then you'll be off into the sunset, without a glimmer of the real affection or unconditional love that you may already have preached are the answers to everything.

Empowerment Ritual
Well, it's hard to be so quirky and yet live a conventional lifestyle, isn't it? This ritual will ensure that you maintain

your spirit, yet help you to accept that others need to know where they stand. During the Waning Moon, place three pieces of amethyst and three of rose quartz in a south corner of your home to boost your love of self, and release the fear of commitment.

Black Moon Lilith in Pisces

Sexual Expression

You are a romantic dreamer and, for you, sex is an escapist experience only found in La-La Land: all sensual, romantic and dreamy. The problem is you're so sensitive to your partner's sexual needs that you often forget or deny that you have any of your own. A sexual artiste, you desire a complete merger of body, mind and soul, where romance is sex, and sex is love, with a lover whose passion and fantasies can blend with your own wilder ones.

Shadow Side

Seductive and easily led astray, you often get involved in superficial flings or one-night stands. You often pick partners who will inevitably disappoint you, because being let down means you can say, 'Well, I knew it all along'. You pay a high price by sacrificing your real sexual needs for the sake of emotional or co-dependent relationships, playing the victim or, at times, the saviour.

Empowerment Ritual

This will bring you awareness of your own sexuality and help you to honour your authentic self. During the Dark of the New Moon, place five red carnelians (or rubies) in a small stone bowl. Light a red candle and take each crystal in turn. Hold close to your Root Chakra and say: 'With this stone, my sexual desire is mine alone; from now on I will never deny it.' Repeat with each crystal, placing them on the table after the affirmation. You will soon be able to express your true desires and liberate yourself from your own illusions.

Conclusion

In closing, here are two quotes from apparently very different, but actually very similar minds. The scientist and the mystic are now thought to be closer to each other in universal awareness than ever before. It seems they have always had the same lunar soul, too.

> *'I like to think that the moon is there even if I am not looking at it.'*
>
> ALBERT EINSTEIN

> *'To see the Moon that cannot be seen,*
> *Turn your eyes inward*
> *And look at yourself . . .*
> *In silence.'*
>
> RUMI

The Moon, whether visible or invisible, eternally moves on through her cycles, and I suppose there will never be a last word from her. But I would like to end this particular little book of her magic by saying this: please go with the flow and energy of the Moon's phases. Listen to your intuition, reconnect to nature's cycles, and learn to make your life what you want it to be. You will soon discover that the Moon's power will bring you what you truly seek.

May the light of the Moon, and the universe, shine through you every day.

# Acknowledgements

My thanks to everyone at Little, Brown who helped to make this book a magical one. I would also like to thank my literary agent, Chelsey Fox, for her eternal support; my family for being who they are and for loving me for who I am; and not forgetting you, the reader, for your belief in the mystical power of the Moon.

Recommended Resources

In order to find out your lunar phase or Moon sign online, you will usually need to enter the time, date and place of your birth. (If you don't know the time, it's best to use midday so you can get an idea of Moon placement.)

Please note, there are many sites offering free birth charts, but they often don't show the horoscope itself, just giving you a reading and asking for other information, like your email address, and so on.

The websites I have listed here are tried and trusted, but of course there may be others that are just as useful, or will appear in the future.

https://horoscopes.astro-seek.com/
birth-chart-horoscope-online

This is the simplest and easiest to use. It includes Black Moon Lilith.

https://astro-charts.com/tools/new/birthchart/

This is very easy to use, but does not include Black Moon Lilith in the basic chart. However, it does tell you which Moon phase you were born under.

https://www.astrotheme.com/horoscope_chart_sign_ascendant.php

This site has a lot of information to digest. It includes Black Moon Lilith.

https://astrolibrary.org/free-birth-chart/

This is an easy site with a very easy calculator. It includes Black Moon Lilith, but there is a lot of blurb to read with the chart.

www.astro.com

Highly recommended for a range of more advanced birth chart data, information and calculations, plus comparison of different charts, planets and asteroids, as well as ephemeris for Black Moon Lilith. You need to know a bit about astrology to work with this site.